Praise for the So

"These are fantast
information and b
inside a backpack".

"Dit is gebruikers
opvoedkundige wa

"Handy travel comp...
literally jam-packed with information ... making these guides
holiday must-haves for an informed and more enjoyable trip"
—*Longevity* magazine

"These handy books are accessible to everyone from the lay person
to geologists and scientists, answering all your questions regarding
these sites"—*Saturday Dispatch*

"... compact pocket guides packed with info, maps and colourful
pictures"—*50/50*

"They are a celebration of various aspects of South African culture,
including our historical inheritance and the land on which we
live"—**Diane de Beer**, *Pretoria News*

"There's this marvellous new collection of pocket guides by
Southbound, each highlighting a specific World Heritage Site in
South Africa ... Easy to use and fun to read, the pocket guides are a
must for anyone remotely interested in our country's heritage"
—*Independent on Saturday*

"These books reveal fascinating parts of our country that many of
us aren't properly aware of. They'd make excellent gifts, singly or
collectively, and are great primers for planning a holiday"
—**Bruce Dennill**, *The Citizen*

"All [eight] of South Africa's World Heritage Sites are covered,
each in a manageable pocket guide which provides a remarkable
amount of information for the edification of the serious ecotourist ...
comprehensive contents ... an extensive amount of information ..."
—**Carol Knoll**, *Environmental Management*

"... intensely practical ... fantastic series to buy ..."
—**Jenny Crwys-Williams**, *Talk Radio 702*

"... these are among the best we have—opinionated and full of
personality"—**Patricia McCracken**, *Farmers Weekly*

About the author

For Allan Davie, it all began with a fascination with dinosaurs at a young age and names like Stegosaurus and Dimetrodon featured large in his vocabulary, leading to degrees in geology from Natal, Rhodes and Leeds universities. He has an enduring interest in the natural world, the evolution of life and Earth history, rivalled by an almost equal passion for travel, having wandered widely on all the continents except Antarctica, which is still an aspiration. He is a contributor of earth-science articles for the *Natal Witness*, publishes a blog titled 'Romancing the Stone' and runs Old Canvas's earth-science workshops for those who might be interested. When he isn't expounding on some aspect of our natural world he enjoys the Natal Midlands life, cold weather and hitting the open road in his trusty old Land Rover.

Published in 2008 by Southbound
An imprint of 30° South Publishers (Pty) Ltd.
28, Ninth Street, Newlands
Johannesburg 2092, South Africa
www.30degreessouth.co.za
info@30degreessouth.co.za

Design, origination & maps by 30° South Publishers (Pty) Ltd.
Printed and bound by Pinetown Printers (Pty) Ltd.

ISBN 978-190143-24-4

Southbound Pocket Guides

The
Whale Trail
of South Africa

Allan Davie

West and southern coast whale trails

N7 to Springbok

N1 to Johannesburg

Lambert's Bay

ATLANTIC
OCEAN

WESTERN CAPE

Beaufort West

Langebaan

Wellington

Worcester

Cape Town

Stellenbosch

George

N2 to Po
Elizabet

Hermanus

Mossel
Bay

Knysna

Cape Agulhas

INDIAN
OCEAN

East coast whale trail

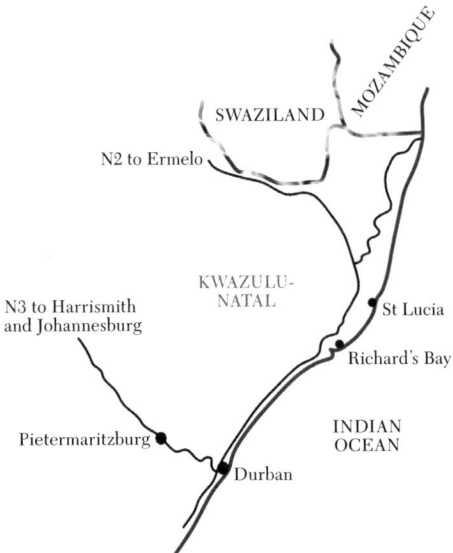

MOZAMBIQUE

SWAZILAND

N2 to Ermelo

KWAZULU-
NATAL

St Lucia

N3 to Harrismith
and Johannesburg

Richard's Bay

INDIAN
OCEAN

Pietermaritzburg

Durban

Contents

Introduction

> "Then the whole world was the whale's; and
> king of creation, he left his wake ..."
> Herman Melville, *Moby Dick*

South Africa offers perhaps the best land-based whale watching on Earth. The scalloped coastline stretching from Saldanha on the west coast to Tsitsikamma in the east provides sheltered waters for southern right whales to calve and mate during the southern winter. Further out to sea, humpback whales make their way to their tropical breeding grounds off the west and east Africa coasts. Humpback and southern right whales are the flagship species of the South African Whale Trail, but all nine of the great whale species are to be found in South African waters, as well as orcas, dolphins and the occasional sperm whale.

The heart of the Whale Trail is at Hermanus, a southern Cape seaside town that fairly oozes 'whaleness'. The whales are by no means confined to Hermanus and are found in all the major embayments of the South African coast. Any visitor to these shores will be seduced by the unbelievable combination of mountains, sea and sky—'*hemel en aarde*' (heaven and earth) in the local vernacular. On sunny days, the air is crisp and clear with visibility to the ends of the earth; on bad days, the sea fog rolls off the littoral, wreathing the mountains in a billowing embrace. On stormy days, the wind whips the spindrift off the breakers and rattles the roof tiles as the surf roars on the shingle. And at all times, the air is full of the intoxicating, aromatic fragrance of the Fynbos and Renosterbos, which grow profusely in the shadows of the mountains. Add to this heady mix the awesome sight of giant whales swimming in the bottle-green rollers, which march in from the South Atlantic, and one cannot help but indulge in the language of the superlative when describing this coastline.

Why do whales have this fascination for mankind? This is a difficult one, but there are few who have heard the deep, echoing breath of these leviathans, or seen a fully grown humpback breaching, and not been moved by the magnificence of these creatures. Man has had an association with Cetaceans dating back to the time of the ancients—an association it must be said that has been almost completely one-sided and to the long-term detriment of whales across the globe. In 2007, a 50-ton bowhead whale was killed by Inuit hunters off the Alaskan coast. The loss of such a magnificent animal is a sad tale, but what makes this story even more tragic is that the creature is estimated to have been between 115 and 130 years old. A fragment of a bomb lance was discovered in its neck that dated back to 1890 and for over a hundred years it had survived with a 9cm harpoon buried under its blubber. Ordinarily, the calculation of a whale's age is based on the level of amino acids in the whale's eye lenses and to discover a whale over a century old is a rare event indeed. The bowhead is estimated to have been born in approximately 1877, around the time Thomas Edison was busy inventing the phonograph. Two years later came the battle of Isandlwana and Rorke's Drift, 1901 saw the passing of Queen Victoria, 1918 the commencement of World War I, 1939 the outbreak of World War II, and 2007 the whale's demise. It is a strange thought that this creature had shared our planet for periods in excess of the lifespan of any human being, and that it had lived through some of worst excesses that we were able to generate in our chequered history.

This story somehow adds to the mystique of these creatures—their lives span large swathes of our immediate past, and yet they are so very distant in terms of the aquatic world, which they inhabit, and which we find almost inaccessible. Migrations to cold, forbidding seas, with only whale song to communicate, instils in the minds of men a sense of wonder at the lives of whales.

Quick facts

Largest whale: The blue whale is the heaviest and longest animal on Earth. The average adult length is 25m (82ft) in males and 26.2m (86ft) in females, with body weights of 90–120 tonnes. Adult blues are known to reach 30m or more.

Smallest: Hector's dolphin is the world's smallest Cetacean. They reach only 1.2m (3.6ft) long when fully grown. The finless porpoise is probably the lightest, weighing 30–45kg (66–70lbs)—it would take nearly 3,000 finless porpoises to balance the scales against a single blue whale.

Tallest blow: A 'blow' or 'spout' is the cloud of water vapour produced when a whale exhales. The tallest blow belongs to the blue whale where blows of up to 12m (40ft) have been reported.

Largest appetite: A blue whale eats up to four tonnes of krill every day, which is the equivalent of eating a fully grown African elephant.

Longest dive: Early whalers reported dive times of more than two hours for northern bottlenose whales.

Deepest dive: The sperm whale is believed to dive deeper than any other Cetacean, with dives as deep as 2,000m (6,560ft) having been recorded.

Longest lived: One bowhead whale was reported to have been 130 years old when it died, based on a harpoon found in its flesh dating back to 1890.

Heaviest brain: The sperm whale has the world's heaviest brain, which can weigh up to 9.2kg (20lb 5oz). Compare this to the average 1.4kg (3lb 1oz) for the brain of an adult human.

Tallest dorsal fin: The huge dorsal fin of a bull orca (killer whale) can reach the remarkable height of 1.8m (6ft)—roughly as tall as a man.

Fastest swimmer: A bull orca has been timed swimming at 55kph (34mph) in the eastern North Pacific.

Most endangered: The baiji, or Chinese river dolphin, is the rarest dolphin in the world. It lives in the Yangtze River in China where there are thought to be perhaps less than 100 of these dolphins remaining. The damming of the river may mean that the dolphin will become extinct in the next few years. The vaquita, a porpoise that lives in the Gulf of California, is the rarest marine dolphin, with only a few hundred surviving.

Whaling decimated the populations of large

whales and today just 300 northern right whales remain, living off the east coast of North America, with dire prospects for recovery of the species.

Longest song: Male humpback whales sing the longest and most complex songs in the animal kingdom. Each song lasts for half an hour or more and comprises several main components. The aim of the singing is probably to woo females and to frighten off rival males. The songs can be heard underwater hundreds, or even thousands, of miles away.

Longest migration: For a long time the grey whale was believed to undertake the longest known migration of any mammal. Hugging the North American coastline, it swims from its winter breeding grounds in Baja California, Mexico, to its summer feeding grounds in the rich waters of the Bering Sea in the Arctic and back again. This amounts to a total annual distance of 12,000–20,000km (7,452–12,420 miles).

In a grey whale's lifetime of 40 years or more, this is equivalent to a return trip to the moon. In recent years, researchers have begun tracking the migration of humpback whales from Antarctic waters to the equator off Colombia and Costa Rica. One female whale was spotted off the Antarctic Peninsula and then re-sighted five months later off Colombia. Even taking the shortest route this would have been a journey of over 8,400km (5,000 miles).

Did you know?

o Orcas are, in fact, the largest member of the dolphin family.

o Whales and dolphins do not sleep like we do, but rest on the surface of the sea or catnap for a few moments while they are swimming. Each side of the brain takes turns to 'switch off' while the other half stays awake and keeps the animal breathing (which is a voluntary action in Cetaceans).

o When whales and dolphins open their eyes underwater, special greasy tears protect them from the stinging salt.

o The black and white markings on the underside of humpback whale tails are all unique. This enables researchers to tell the whales apart by taking pictures of the tail, which lifts clear of the water as the whale dives. Bottlenose dolphins and orcas can be individually identified from the different markings and nicks on their dorsal fins.

o Cetaceans without teeth are called mysticetes and feed via built-in filters. They have what look like long, furry combs in their mouths called baleen plates, which hang from their upper jaws to form a giant sieve. A baleen whale feeds by taking in large mouthfuls of water and then filtering out all the fish or krill (small shrimp-like organisms that live in the sea) before swallowing the captured prey. It may eat thousands or even hundreds of thousands of organisms in a single gulp.

o The bowhead has longer baleen than any other whale. At 4.5m (15ft) it would be twice the height from ceiling to floor of most modern houses.

Protection of whales

South African Cetaceans are protected under the Marine Resources Act (Act No. 18 of 1998). However, protection is no guarantee of safety and all whale species are subject to man-made hazards including pirate whaling, pollution, ocean dumping and entanglement in fishing lines and nets. In addition, offshore oil exploration, fishing, resort development, military activities and increased boat and ship traffic impact on the aquatic environment and whales and small Cetaceans. Increased boat traffic also includes the activities of boat-based whale watching (BBWW) and there may be evidence that these activities could discourage whales from breeding or interfere with the mother–calf bond. In this light then, any boat-based whale watching operation must have the necessary permits, abide by the regulations of the Marine Living Resources Act of 1998, and be sensitive to the impacts that any operation of this nature may have on the wellbeing of these animals.

On the recommendations of the Dolphin Action and Protection Group, the South African authorities gazetted regulations in 1980 to protect whales from killing, disturbance and harassment. The Sea Fisheries Act has been replaced by the Marine Resources Act (Act No. 18 of 1998) and regulations to protect whales from the same were gazetted once again on 2 September 1998. They read as follows:

1. No person shall, except on the authority of a permit:
   - Engage in fishing, collecting, killing, attempting to kill, disturbing, harassing, keeping or controlling of, or be in the possession of, any whale or any part of product thereof at any time.
   - Operate any whale-watching business that causes a disturbance or harassment of any whale within the meaning of subregulation (2), or
   - Offer his or her services for, or make available his expertise in connection with any of the activities referred to in this subregulation.

2. For the purpose of subregulation (1), 'disturbing or harassing' shall also include:

(a) the shooting of any whale;

(b) approaching closer than 300m to any whale by means of a fishing vessel, vessel, aircraft, or other method; and

(c) that in the event of a whale surfacing closer than 300m from a fishing vessel, vessel, aircraft, the person in charge of such fishing vessel, vessel, or aircraft fails to proceed immediately to a distance of at least 300m from the whale.

Provided that paragraphs (b) and (c) shall not apply to bona fide efforts by any person rendering aid to a beached, entrapped or entangled whale.

Offences and penalties

Any person who contravenes or fails to comply with any provision of these regulations shall be guilty of an offence and liable on conviction to a fine or to imprisonment for a period not exceeding two years.

The slow come-back

'The Cape'—two words that have a particular resonance to many who frequent these shores or who live within spindrift distance of her cold, green waters. All visitors to this coast are seduced by the clarity of the light, the tang of the sea breezes, the ferocity of her storms, and the enveloping fog billowing off the cold sea. It is a world of extremes, where mountains step down to the narrow littoral, which is constantly under the onslaught of long rollers generated by the frontal weather patterns of the Southern Ocean. Wide embayments, their form controlled by the grain of an ancient continent, provide shelter for man and beast along this inhospitable coastline, with rocky promontories with the evocative names of Cape Infanta, Cape Recife and Cape St Francis harking back to the first Portuguese seafarers who explored this coastline. Francis Drake described it as "the fairest Cape in all the circumference of the globe". However, another kind of voyager visits this enchanted coastline, and has been doing so for millennia, way before the tentative explorings of these early seafarers. These voyagers are whales—giant and superb navigators of the world's oceans. Since time immemorial, they have made their way from cold Antarctic seas to the relative warmth and safety of the Cape coast to breed and nurse their young, and to avoid the rigours of the Southern Ocean winters.

We take delight in this annual migration, and this coastline provides perhaps the finest land-based whale watching on Earth. However, those bipedal beings that inhabit the terrestrial world have not always made it hospitable for these leviathans, with whaling stations straddling the coastline in a bloody arc from Durban on the east coast to Saldanha Bay on the west. Fifty million years of evolution was almost undone by a mere 300 years of ruthless slaughter, which continued unabated until someone realized that whale populations were severely depleted and, without intervention, were in danger of being destroyed completely. In this light an international convention was held in 1946 to regulate the whaling industry, from which the International Whaling Commission (IWC) was brought into being. Unbelievably, there is still no international law protecting whales, the only international regulations being those of the IWC. IWC or not, the slaughter continued in South Africa until 1976, which saw the last whaling operations in South African waters. This was due to the collapse of whale populations along the coast, with attendant low returns on investments, rather than a change of heart. Only in 2001, thanks to the ongoing campaign by the Dolphin Action and Protection Group, did the South

African government change its policy on commercial whaling and stop supporting the lethal exploitation of whales. Since the mid-seventies, whale stocks have slowly clawed back lost ground and 3,000 of the 9,000 southern right whales on Earth today migrate to the South African coastline each year. They come without fear of disturbance and in doing so provide us with phenomenal whale watching during the South African winter. Further out to sea, humpback whales head north to their tropical breeding grounds off the west and east African coast. Other members of the Cetacea, dolphins and porpoises, make this coastline their home and few who have spent time on the beaches have not thrilled to the sight of a school of dolphins surfing the waves, or leaping in vast schools out on the wider ocean.

This then is an invitation to spend time on this coastline, to enjoy first and foremost the incredible spectacle of whales in the bays, but also to partake in the rich historical and cultural heritage of this region. All this is set against the vistas of mountains and sea, which provide the backdrop for one of the most amazing experiences on Earth.

Whales of the Whale Trail

All of the nine great whale species of the southern hemisphere are represented in South Africa's coastal zone. However, only the southern right whale comes close inshore and as a result is the most familiar to whale watchers along our coastline.

Southern right whales (*Eubalaena australis*)

'Southern' because they occur in the southern hemisphere, and 'right' because they provided high yields of oil and blubber and were kind enough to float once killed. These attributes were almost their undoing, making these slow-moving whales vulnerable to hunting. Thanks to the enthusiastic endeavours of several generations of whalers, southern right whales are still on the near-threatened list, although numbers are increasing at seven percent per year, equating to a doubling of populations every ten years. The species was granted international protection in 1935 and South Africa provides sanctuary to an estimated 3,000 of the 9,000 southern right whales currently populating the southern oceans. However, this is no reason for complacency as it is estimated that populations are but ten percent of the initial stocks before whaling started in earnest in the eighteenth century.

The southern right whale has a circumpolar distribution and inhabits sub-Antarctic waters between 30° and 55°S. Seasonal migration takes them southward during the summer months when krill supplies are more abundant, and north in the winter months to mate, calve and rear their young. The season for southern rights is from May to December, although they have been sighted as early as April and as late as February. They gather in the sheltered bays of the Cape coast and it is this behaviour which makes them so easy to watch and, in days gone by, to kill.

Identification

Although not the largest whales in the sea, their size is still impressive, with adult females ranging in length from 12.4m to 15.5m (40ft to 47ft) with an average of 13.9m (42ft). Estimated weights are in the region of 29 to 58 tonnes based on figures derived from northern right whales of similar lengths. The males are generally slightly smaller than the females. Tail flukes are similarly impressive, reaching spans ranging from 4.3m (13ft) to 5.7m (17ft) across in mature adults. Flippers are supported by skeletons, which hark back to the days of land mammals and are squareish in outline. The dorsal fin is absent.

Distinctive callosities allow for easy identification of southern right whales from other species and provide a method of recognizing particular individuals in a population group. Callosities are pale brown growths of horny skin on the whale's head, their locations corresponding to positions of rudimentary hairs. A V-shaped blow also distinguishes this whale from the other whales along our coastline, the V due to two nostrils or blow holes on the whale's head.

Behaviour

Southern right whale behaviour is perhaps the most studied due to the numbers of whales that over-winter along South Africa's coastline. Breaching, lobtailing, spyhopping and sailing are all part of the southern right whale's repertoire and are what delights both land and boat-based whale watchers alike. Southern right whales swim at speeds of 0.5kph (0.3mph) to 4kph (2.5mph) with top speeds in the order of 17kph (11mph). The whale makes dives of four to eight minutes duration, although longer dives may take place in the open ocean.

In coastal waters, the whales produce a range of low-frequency sounds (less than 1,000Hz), the repertoire comprising moans, growls, pulses and belch-like noises. Clearly a form of communication between individuals, different sounds relate to different activities.

Data derived from the logbooks of nineteenth-century whalers give valuable insights into the migration patterns of whales. Information on geographical position, whales killed and processed, and myriad irrelevant but interesting details as they followed the whale herds allowed for a picture to be built up of migration routes. The records show that during the summer months the southern right whales migrate from coastal waters to the region of the Subtropical Convergence Zone located at approximately 42°S, where they spend December and January. From there they migrate further south to between 45°S and 50°S from February to April, following which they begin the long migration back to the South African coastline, arriving here in May to mate and calve.

Feeding

Southern right whales are mysticete (baleen) whales and feed by taking in quantities of prey and seawater and separating the food by filtering it through the baleen plates that extend from the roof of the mouth. The whales' main diet in the Southern Ocean is copepods—a type of plankton—which reach lengths of only a few millimetres but which occur in dense swarms. If the swarm is located near the surface, the whale will plough back and forth with open mouth in a lawnmower-like action, filtering out the food through the baleen plates. Every so often they close their mouths to swallow the accumulated plankton. Copepods may also be concentrated around a thermocline or the sea floor, and it is assumed that the whales have a technique of feeding from these deeper accumulations, although no one has yet observed this behaviour. It is estimated that a southern right whale will consume between 600kg (1,300lbs) and 1,600kg (3,500lbs) of food per day during the feeding period, as they accumulate fat and blubber for the long summers in coastal waters where feeding is at a minimum.

Breeding

Mating is thought to take place within the sheltered embayments of our coastline. Roughly equal numbers of male and female calves are born, but with the drawback from a male point of view that approximately one-third of mature females are ready to mate in any year. With ratios like this, there is a surplus of males to females in the population. Whale watchers may see a group of whales engaged in frolicking and boisterous interplay at the surface, with whale bodies rolling and flippers waving skywards, combined with much blowing and puffing. It is thought that these antics are part of the mating game, where several males will compete for the attentions of a female. During this fairly unromantic courtship, the males circle and caress the female, who often plays coy and takes evasive action by fleeing into the shallows or by lying on the surface on her back. Mating is thought to be quick, but frequent, and may involve all the males in the group, the strategy being one of sperm competition, whereby each male attempts to dilute the sperm of his predecessor, thereby reducing his chances of fertilizing the female. The ability to produce large volumes of sperm is clearly an advantage in this competitive situation and huge testes of up to 500kg each have been recorded in northern right whales and one can assume their southern cousins are similarly endowed. No lasting bonds develop between cows and the males due to this strategy, and the males play no further role in the rearing of the young. Gestation is approximately a year, which allows for enough time for a Southern Ocean feeding cycle before returning to coastal waters to calve. The calves range from 5m (15ft) to 6m (18ft) at birth and strong bonds exist between the mothers and their young.

Status and protection

The southern right whale's status is near-threatened under the IUCN Red List of Threatened Species. The northern right whale is virtually extinct, a fate that may have befallen its southern hemisphere cousins if some measures had not been put in place to protect the species. Complete protection was accorded to all right whales in 1935, but it took several years before South Africa ceased southern right whaling, legislation being passed eventually in 1940, which almost stopped the killing. However, a few were taken right into the 1950s, undeclared of course. Since the 1970s, populations have been increasing at seven percent a year, which is a remarkable and heartening return from the edge of oblivion. However, the South African population is thought to be only ten percent of the original population levels which existed in the seventeenth century when the first Europeans came to the Cape.

Humpback whales (*Megaptera novaeangliae*)

The whalers out of New England gave this species their name—big-winged New Englander—due to the enormous length of its flippers, which grow to almost a third of its body length. They are also known for their ability to sing, with male humpbacks singing the longest and most complex songs in the animal kingdom. Each song may last for half an hour and comprises several main components, with the singing thought to attract females and to discourage rival males. Theirs is truly the song of the deep, where the sounds can travel hundreds, and at times thousands, of miles beneath the waves.

Humpback whales occur in all the oceans of the world

and migrate to colder, high-latitude waters during the summer months, but return to tropical and subtropical seas during the Antarctic winter. Annual migrations of up to 25,000km are typical, making it one of the best-travelled of any mammalian species. Humpback whales seen off the South African coast are generally en route to breeding grounds off west and east Africa, as well as the Indian Ocean islands and as such they do not linger long in the bays along our coast.

Identification

They are members of the rorqual family, with characteristic pleats of grooves on the underside of the throat and chest, which allow for expansion of the mouth area during feeding. The body is relatively short and round compared to other rorquals (including blue, fin, sei and minke whales), and the exceptionally long, pure white flippers characterize the species. Knobbly tubercles occur on the broad, round head and along the margin of the jaws. The flippers may reach lengths of 5m (16ft) in mature females. Humpbacks grow to sizes ranging from 14.6m (48ft) to 15.2m (50ft) for males and females respectively, with weights averaging 30,000kg (66,000lbs) to 40,000kg (88,000lbs) for both sexes. Colouration is very dark grey with white areas covering the throat grooves and ventral area. The dorsal fin is small and triangular shaped, and is located approximately two-thirds of the way along the back, and is mounted on a distinctive fleshy platform. The flukes are serrated on their trailing edges and the variable white patterns on the underside are peculiar to each individual, allowing for identification and observation of their migratory patterns. Similarly to southern rights, their flippers are supported on relic skeletons, indicating a terrestrial origin for their evolution.

Behaviour

The blow is pear-shaped, upright and reaches a height of approximately 3m (10ft). They are slow swimmers, with average speeds of approximately 8kph (5mph). On diving, they raise their tail flukes clear of the water. This shows off the serrations on their tail flukes and white markings, which assists in specific identification of individuals. Breaching is another behavioural characteristic of humpback whales where they throw almost two-thirds of their body length clear of the water in an arching back flip, falling back with a tremendous splash. On occasions, they also may be seen rolling on the surface, slapping the water with their flukes or flippers, or lying on their sides holding one flipper in the air.

Feeding

Antarctic humpback whales feed almost exclusively on krill. They feed at or near the surface using a variety of techniques, including horizontal lunging, circular swimming and thrashing 'flick feeding' in which the fluke is used to stun or concentrate the prey. Then there is bubble feeding, whereby submerged whales release large clouds of bubbles, which 'fence' in schools of fish or plankton.

Breeding and gestation

Gestation lasts approximately 13 months and the normal reproduction cycle for humpbacks appears to be two or three years. Lactation lasts almost a year. Calves are approximately 4.5m (15ft) long at birth.

Status

The humpback whale is listed as 'vulnerable' under the IUCN Red List of Threatened Species. The proximity of their migration routes to the coastline, as well as their slow-swimming habits, have made them vulnerable to hunting forays from those destructive inhabitants of the terrestrial world—man. The IWC declared a ban on commercial killing of humpbacks in the North Atlantic in 1955, the North Pacific in 1965 and the southern hemisphere in 1966. Since its low point at the time of the 1966 moratorium, populations have increased to about 38,000 today, with estimated North Atlantic populations at 11,600 animals, and 10,000 and 17,000 for the North Pacific and southern hemisphere respectively. Apart from a small quota for aboriginal peoples, the humpback is currently a fully protected species. Scientific research indicates that their numbers are increasing at or near to the absolute maximum rate, but numbers are still below original population levels prior to the commencement of commercial whaling on a large scale. Protection is no guarantee of safety, however, and all whale species are subject to man-made hazards including pirate whaling, pollution, ocean dumping and entanglement in fishing lines and nets.

Bryde's whales (*Balaenoptera edeni*)

Norwegian businessman Johan Bryde established the South African Whaling Company whaling station in the port of Durban in 1908, expanding the company's interests to include the whaling station at Donkergat, Saldanha, in 1909. In 1912, he financed the first study of whales in South African waters, which led to the discovery of a new species, which was named after Mr Bryde. Up until then, Bryde's whales had been confused with sei whales, which they resemble.

Population numbers are not known to any degree of certainty and as such it is difficult to estimate the species' status in terms of whether it is threatened or not. Apparently, three populations of Bryde's whales exist off the South African coastline. The first is to be found over the continental shelf, south of approximately 30°S.

Most of this population occurs between Cape Agulhas and Port Elizabeth during the summer months, with a tendency to migrate around the Cape to the west coast during winter. One of the other populations, known as the South East Atlantic Stock, occurs on the west coast and extends from the equator to approximately 34°S, migrating northwards during autumn and southwards in the spring. The third, less well-studied population, is found in some numbers south of Madagascar. Whales from the inshore and offshore populations have variations in size, scarring, baleen shape and reproductive behaviour.

They do occasionally come close inshore, but their movements are unpredictable, which is probably a function of food sources and fish migration patterns. Whale watchers may spot them in Walker Bay, False Bay and Plettenberg Bay quite close to the shore, but there is more chance of sightings out on the open sea.

Identification

Female Bryde's whales are larger than the males, reaching lengths of 14.6m (48ft), with an average length of 13m (39ft), while the males reach lengths of 14.3m (43ft) with an average length of 12m (36ft). They weigh in at 12 tonnes with a maximum recorded weight of 20 tonnes. The body is slender and the top of the head, the rostrum, appears broad and flat when viewed from above. Rorquals have a distinctive median ridge, which runs from the blow hole to the tip of the snout. Bryde's whales have the same arrangement, but with an additional two extra ridges, which makes for easier identification of the species. Baleen plates number approximately 300 on either side of the top jaw and are generally less than 45cm (18in) in length, which is short by whale standards. The dorsal fin (that's the one on the back) stands 45cm tall and is located two-thirds of the way towards the tail. It is more erect and pointed than the humpback whale and may show fraying or notching along the trailing edge. The flippers are slender and pointed, and are about ten percent of total body length.

Behaviour

Observations by the Dolphin Action and Protection Group (DAPG) over a period of nine years have shown that Bryde's whales are not overly gregarious, with most sightings being of individual animals or of a pair. However, larger feeding aggregations do occur and they have been known to follow large schools of fish in association with other marine mammals, particularly dolphins, as well as seals and seabirds. They have also been seen associated with southern right whales and the two species co-exist without interfering with one another. They appear unafraid of vessels and will approach small craft and at times will accompany the vessels for some distance.

They are deep divers and on surfacing expose their head followed by a large expanse of back and a humping movement of the tail. They seldom show their flukes. The blow is tall and thin, reaching heights of 4m (13ft), but the blow is not clearly visible from a distance. Swimming speeds range from eight to 32kph.

Feeding

Bryde's whales are rorquals, and they are able to gulp large mouthfuls of food and seawater in an efficient cycle of gulping and straining of seawater, keeping the residual fish, squid or krill on their baleen plates. They have been observed feeding on shoals of fish, which have been penned in and driven to the surface by other predators, and are approached by the whales from below. The whales surface on their sides with mouths open, which allows them to take in vast mouthfuls of fish, following which they then roll upright, blow and submerge. Whether this behaviour is typical of normal feeding methods has not yet been established.

Breeding
Breeding occurs year round with an average gestation period of 12 months. The calf has an average mass of 1,000kg (2,200lbs) and is approximately 4m (12ft) in length. Sexual maturity occurs at ten years for males and eight years for females.

Status and protection
In South African waters, 1,564 Bryde's whales were taken between 1917 and 1967 from shore-based whaling stations. However, some caution needs to be exercised as the species may not have been distinguished from sei whales, which they closely resemble. In 1977, Japan Far Seas Fisheries Research Laboratory assigned itself a scientific permit to kill 240 Bryde's whales in the Southern Ocean to 'estimate' the population, size and structure of this zero-quota stock for rational exploitation. The scientific permit was worth at the time $3,600,000. Since 2000, Japan has been killing Bryde's whales in the North Pacific for so-called scientific research. This programme has received much criticism from IWC member countries. During the 1970s, a pirate whaler, MV *Sierra*, killed some 1,500 Bryde's whales off the west coast of South Africa, all of which were sold to Japan. There are few estimates of Bryde's whale population sizes, and no data on how many Bryde's whales there were before the killing began. During the 1980s, scientists counted inshore stock of Bryde's whales on the South African coast during January and February, and 156 Bryde's whales were sighted between East London and the Orange River mouth. Research shows that there is only a discreet population of Bryde's whales that are resident inshore in

certain areas off the South African coast, and which need continued monitoring and protection.

Killer whales (*Orcinus orca*)

Actually a member of the dolphin species, the killer whale, or orca, is an infrequent visitor to our shores, although sightings are made throughout the year. Much maligned in the past as a predatory killer with a treacherous temperament, these myths have been disproved thanks to ongoing studies and scientific research. Granted, the species is the only Cetacean to live on warm-blooded animals, but there are absolutely no recorded instances anywhere in the world of unprovoked attacks on human beings by killer whales. Some of you may have seen the David Attenborough series, *The Trials of Life*, where cameramen Mike de Gruy and Paul Atkins, suited up and lying in the surf zone, waited for an orca to take one of the numerous sea lion cubs that were on the beach. One wonders what their thoughts were during the wait and of course at the moment of truth when the orca came up the beach. Were they going to be the first victim of an unprovoked attack by a killer whale? Happily, all went according to plan, they got some great footage and the cameramen covered themselves in glory.

Orcas are to be found worldwide, but population levels are higher in the Arctic and Antarctic waters. In some regions, they appear to be migratory, while in others are apparently present all year round. They have been sighted around the coasts of South Africa, Namibia and Mozambique during all months of the year. Sightings range from the surf zone to 600km (375 miles) out to sea, although numbers aren't prolific in our waters.

Identification

Thanks to plenty of media coverage and recent films, few can mistake the distinctive black, white and grey markings of the orca. Most animals have a light-grey saddle marking just behind the dorsal fin, the shape varying between individuals and providing a useful means of identifying different individuals. Another distinctive feature is their dorsal fin, which in mature males is a whopping 1.7m (5.1ft) tall and is easily recognizable from a fair distance away. In females and immature males, the dorsal fin is about half this height. The norm is reversed in these species, where the male is larger than the female, reaching lengths of 9m (27ft), while the females may be a full metre shorter. Fully grown orcas weigh in at just over seven tonnes.

Behaviour

Orcas travel in pods, which can number up to 50 animals, although larger groups have been recorded, particularly in Antarctic waters. Pod cohesion is high, with males, females and calves travelling together throughout the year. They travel in contact with one another, either close together or along a broad front, which generally doesn't exceed 1.2km (0.75 miles). There is a high degree of co-operation, particularly when hunting, and there is much evidence for communal concern within the pod.

Orcas are capable of swimming at speeds of 50kph (31mph), which is phenomenal, and can dive to depths in excess of 300m (1,000ft). They frequently spyhop, which enables them to view what is happening above the surface, breach spectacularly and lobtail. Sonar gets them around, allows them to communicate with one another and, perhaps most importantly, is indispensable for locating their prey.

Feeding

Orcas appear to be opportunistic feeders and diet may vary from one region to the next within a specific area. They are primarily fish eaters but also feed on cephalopods as well as other Cetaceans, seals and seabirds. They appear to be selective in their choice and timing of food intake—when hunting they will shun a particular food source in preference of another. This would indicate that they are not wanton or opportunistic killers.

Breeding

Not much is known about the orca's breeding habits. Calves have been observed throughout the year, which indicates that mating takes place throughout the year and is not confined to a particular breeding season. A female can calve every three to five years, and the gestation period is approximately 13 to 17 months. At birth, the calves are around 1.8 to 2.1m (6 to 7ft) long and weigh in at 180kg (400lbs).

Orcas reach sexual maturity at ages ranging from ten to 18 years and the females are reproductively active until their early forties.

Status and protection

Orcas have been harvested worldwide, including in South Africa, but on a relatively small scale. In the 1979/1989 Antarctic whaling season, the then Soviet Union caught 906 killer whales, which led to the IWC banning factory-ship whaling of this species. It takes approximately 5.6 killer whales to produce the same oil yield as one sperm whale, and the meat is considered unfit for human consumption. Several countries now have regulations to protect Cetaceans with their 200 nautical mile exclusive economic zone, but there was (and still is) little international legislation to protect small Cetaceans, including orcas. They remain vulnerable to hunting, entanglement and habitat destruction. However, since 2003, the IWC has set up some systems to tackle the many threats to small Cetaceans and not just the commercially valuable whale species.

Dolphins

This guide would not be complete without a treatise on dolphins. Throughout the long history of man's association with the sea, the dolphin has attained mythical status and features large in Hellenic and Roman mythology as well as in aboriginal and European folklore. The Homeric Hymns recount how Poseidon used a dolphin to find Amphitrite whom he wanted as his wife. She, however, wasn't keen on this idea and had been hiding in a cavern beneath the waves. After finding her, Poseidon showed his gratitude by setting in the night sky the constellation of the dolphin—Delphinus. Then there are the stories of dolphins rescuing men. Herodotus, in the fifth century BC, recounts how Arion, a famous musician, charters a ship to transport him and his riches home to Corinth. The crew, of course, have designs on the treasure in the hold, and once out on the open sea give him the option to either kill himself or throw himself into the sea. With the odds stacked against him, and failing to strike up a bargain with his captors, they allow him to play one last song on the quarterdeck of the ship. This song is so beguiling that it attracts a dolphin, and with the fading of the last notes he throws himself into the sea. The waiting dolphin carries him to safety on its back, and on his return to Corinth, Arion recounts the story of the crew's treachery to King Periander. On their arrival, the crew swear that they left Arion alive and well in Italy, but the game is up and justice meted out accordingly. The theme of dolphins rescuing sailors is a recurring one, and another account by Plutarch tells how a native of the Greek island of Paros pleaded for the lives of some dolphins, which had been caught by fishermen. Some time later, on a voyage between Paros and Naxos the ship foundered in a storm, and he, alone of all the crew, survived, rescued by a dolphin, which carried him back to the shore.

Myth and mystery aside, few cannot thrill to the beauty of a school of dolphins in full cry across the glassy swells, or delight in the antics of a school surfing in the bottle-green breakers. Dolphins, like whales, are warm-blooded mammals, give birth to live young and by all accounts are blessed with great intelligence. They are part of the toothed-whale family, which includes the sperm whale. Orcas, or killer whales, are also members of the dolphin family. There are 79 species of whales known to science—12 are baleen whales, and the rest are toothed, and 37 dolphin and whale species have been recorded in South African waters. Porpoises, however, do not occur along our coastline, in spite of the fact that dolphins are often mistakenly called porpoises. The major difference between the two species is that porpoises have spade-shaped teeth, while dolphins have conical teeth.

Dolphins are highly streamlined, an obvious evolutionary advantage for living in the oceans. They are amongst the fastest swimmers in the sea, attaining speeds in excess of 30kph (19mph). Powerful muscles in the back and belly of the dolphin, far larger than in similarly sized land animals, provide the propulsive power that drives the flukes, which give the dolphins their exceptional speed. In addition, soft, oily skin reduces drag and therefore propulsive effort required to drive the animal forward. Speed and an ability to dive to depth are imperative in the quest for food. Dive times and depths vary considerably between species and depend also on the depths at which their quarry lives. Bottlenose dolphins, which are common along the South African coastline, can dive for periods of up to eight minutes although about 30 seconds is the average time. They probably never dive deeper than 40m (120ft), which is not much greater than a sport diver. Sperm whales, being of the same toothed whale family, can dive for up to 90 minutes and to depths of more than 1,000m (300ft), which is quite astounding. Dolphins take about two seconds to expel their stale air through their blow holes and inhale fresh air before submerging again. Sense of smell is nonexistent in dolphins, although apparently they do have a well-developed sense of taste. They are also sensitive to touch.

As any diver will tell you, visibility in water, as compared to air, is reduced, with 10 to 20 metres in even very clear water being considered exceptional. With limited visibility, dolphins need other methods to find their way around and here is the marvellous part— they, like whales, have developed underwater 'sonar' or echolocation, which they use to create an auditory 'picture' of their surroundings much like bats do in air. Sounds are generated by passing air through various passages in the head, these sounds being reflected out of the dish-shaped skull as a wavefront.

Any object in the range of these sound waves reflects the signal back to the dolphin. These reflections are received through the lower jaw and passed to the ears. The ears are incredibly sensitive, able to pick up sound frequencies six times that of humans. The reflected sounds are converted to nerve impulses and relayed to the brain, which then processes the information and directs the dolphin's actions. The auditory 'picture' provides information on shape, size and direction of movement of an object in the water. It is so sensitive that the dolphin can tell the difference between a 50mm (2in) and a 45mm diameter sphere located 25m (75ft) away. This, to say the least, is phenomenal.

Dolphins live on fish and squid, which they catch individually and swallow whole. Killer whales eat penguins but have been known to pack and hunt other dolphins, whales or seals. Dolphins also co-operate in catching prey, whereby a group will surround a school of fish and take turns to gorge on the encircled fish. High metabolisms, due to the need to constantly surface to breathe and hunt, requires large quantities of food, and typically a bottlenose dolphin will consume six percent of its body mass per day, which for a 130kg (290lbs) animal equates to 9kg (20lbs) of fish and squid.

Dolphin courtship includes enthusiastic leaping, speed swimming and other acrobatic acts, which is then followed by actual mating. Gestation lasts between eight and 16 months depending on the size and species of the animal. Females bear a single calf underwater, with the calf's tail exiting first. If, as in the case of most terrestrial animals, the head were to exit first, the calf would have a good chance of drowning. The calf is perfectly able to swim and in many of the births witnessed in captivity, a midwife dolphin has escorted the youngster to the surface to take its first breath. Whether this behaviour is common in the wild is not known, because births at sea have only rarely been observed. Soon after birth, the calf suckles for the first time. The watery realm adds additional challenges to nursing a young baby. The calf has to suckle between breaths, each feed taking approximately 15 seconds. When wanting to feed, the calf nudges the mammary area and the mother ejects her teat, which the calf takes into its mouth. The mother then actively pumps milk out as the calf swallows, which ensures that the calf gets all the available milk from the mother. The milk is very rich in fat, approximately four times that of human milk, which allows the calf to grow very quickly. Calves suckle for up to 18 months, although they start to take solids after approximately six months.

Most dolphins reach full size after 12 years, and reach ages of at least 20 years and in some cases over 30 years.

Dolphins of the South African coastline

	Dusky dolphin	Bottlenose dolphin	Common dolphin	Fraser's dolphin	Heaviside's dolphin	Risso's dolphin	Humpback dolphin	Southern right whale dolphin
Length (m)	Up to 2m	Up to 3.7m	Up to 2.6m	Up to 2.6m	Up to 1.7m	Up to 3.5m	Up to 2m	Up to 1.8m
Snout and body characteristics	Pointed but no defined beak.	Short snout.	Beak long, narrow, well defined. Two distinct forms recognized—the short beaked and the long beaked.	Very short, stubby snout, robust body.	Snout pointed, no defined beak.	Head rounded, no beak in prominent crease in forehead. Body robust in front of dorsal fin, tapering off to narrow tailstock.	Beak long and slender. Robust body. Distinctive hump on back with roughly triangular fin mounted on top.	Body streamlined.

	Dusky dolphin	Bottlenose dolphin	Common dolphin	Fraser's dolphin	Heaviside's dolphin	Risso's dolphin	Humpback dolphin	Southern right whale dolphin
Colouring and distinctive markings	Black above, white below, two colours sharply defined but varying in extent. Black streak from base of flipper to eye.	Not directly pigmented. Dark grey back, white belly. Indian Ocean and Atlantic species differ slightly.	Dark back, white belly. Salient features are two elongated lens-shaped light areas defining a 'figure of eight' appearance.	Dark grey/blue above, pinkish white below, with two parallel stripes running full length of the body. Upper stripe pale, lower stripe blackish grey.	Black, grey and white. When viewed from above, the dorsal pattern appears only as a narrow black saddle between fin and forehead.	Uniform dark grey at birth but fades with age, becoming almost white on face, belly and back directly before the dorsal fin. Considerable colour variation but all animals laced with fine white scars.	Deep grey with lighter belly. Calves pale cream. White blazes on tips of beak and flippers in older animals.	Body black and white. Snout and flippers white.

36

	Dusky dolphin	Bottlenose dolphin	Common dolphin	Fraser's dolphin	Heaviside's dolphin	Risso's dolphin	Heaviside's dolphin	Humpback dolphin	Southern right whale dolphin
Flippers, flukes and dorsal fins	Flippers and flukes pointed and black on both surfaces. Dorsal fin moderate in size and concave; black, although lighter towards the trailing edge.	Recurved dorsal fin in middle of back.	Tail region very slender. Dorsal fin recurved and in middle of back.	Small dorsal fin, hooked at tip.	Flippers oval shaped and black. Dorsal fin broadly triangular.	Flippers long and pointed. Dorsal fin very tall and curved, similar to bottlenose dolphin.		Flippers short and rounded.	No dorsal fin.

	Dusky dolphin	Bottlenose dolphin	Common dolphin	Fraser's dolphin	Heaviside's dolphin	Risso's dolphin	Humpback dolphin	Southern right whale dolphin
Location	Found only in southern hemisphere.	Occur along both Atlantic and Indian Ocean coastlines, often close inshore surfing in the breakers.	Common around the South African coastline.	Found mainly on South African east coast, associated with warm water.	Found only on west coast of South Africa, from Cape Peninsula northwards, possibly as far north as Angola/Namibia	Found mostly in deep water in tropical and warm temperate regions, including the South African coastline.	They are known to occur inshore along the eastern and south-eastern coast. Possibly declining in South African waters.	Frequent southern and sub-Antarctic oceans.

Southbound Pocket Guides

	Dusky dolphin	Bottlenose dolphin	Common dolphin	Fraser's dolphin	Heaviside's dolphin	Risso's dolphin	Humpback dolphin	Southern right whale dolphin
Behaviour	Comes close to shore in subgroups of one to 200. Groups of 600 have been recorded out to sea. Associates with boats and rides their bow waves.	Often seen close inshore in schools and subgroups surfing in the breakers.	Most likely to be seen in large groups out to sea. They enjoy swimming in wake of ships or bow riding.	Aggressive swimmers, swim adjacent to vessels, leaping energetically. Seen in large schools of up to 500. Oceanic.	Travels in small groups and appears to stay close inshore. Larger schools seen offshore. Associates with boats and bow rides.	Usually seen in groups of three to 30 in deep water. Known to mass strand.	A coastal species, usually congregating in groups of two to 20.	Usually swims in schools of 30 to 100 but schools estimated up to 1,000 have been recorded.

Whale theatrics

Whales spend much of their time swimming, which is only appropriate for an animal that is confined to a watery realm. However, this swimming includes some slightly fancier antics, which liven up the show, and perhaps the lives of these leviathans. If you are fortunate, you may get to see some of the more spectacular whale behaviour during your whale-watching expeditions and these various behavioural patterns are discussed below.

Breaching

Perhaps the most spectacular is breaching and there can be few sights as magnificent as a 30-tonne humpback or southern right whale launching itself out of the water in a streaming, arching leap, before falling onto its back or side with a fantastic splash. Frequently, several breaches occur in succession, although why they do this is uncertain, but it has been postulated that it might be to dislodge parasites, as a means of communication or as a display for other whales nearby. But it may be for no other reason than pure, unadulterated fun. I like the latter theory.

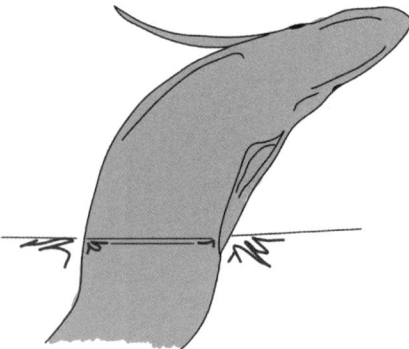

Sailing

The classic images of whale tails are generally taken when a whale is sailing. The whale will 'stand on its head' with its tail protruding above the water for long periods. Again, no one is sure why they do this, but like everything else, several theories have been put forward to explain the behaviour. One is that there might be some kind of heat exchange whereby it picks up solar radiation or cools via evaporation, as blood vessels in the tail form a counter-current system much like a radiator. Another is that the whale might literally be sailing, allowing the wind to push it through the water. The final theory is that it might be feeding on organisms close to the sea floor.

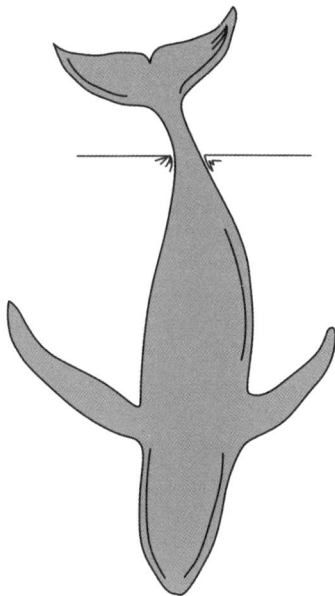

Lobtailing

Almost as an addendum to the sailing manoeuvre, the whales often slap their tails on the water with a loud slap and shower of spray. This lobtailing may take place over long periods and the reasons again are speculative, although it may represent a form of communication, alarm, annoyance or mild threat.

Spyhopping

The whales sometimes stand vertically in the water with their heads protruding above the surface. Although no one has ever seen through a whale's eye, it is thought that they might have reasonable vision in air as well as in water, and spyhopping may well be nothing more than having a look at what is going on in the non-watery world. Calves will spyhop in response to a circling helicopter, when they will follow the movement of the aircraft, indicating at least some visual connection with the non-aquatic world above.

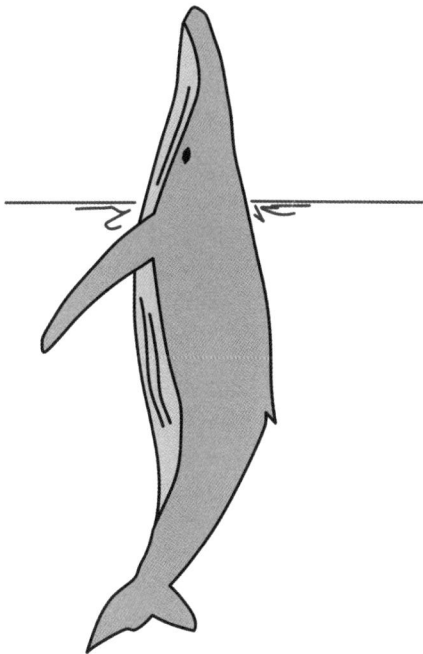

Playing with kelp

Large kelp forests thrive in the cold waters of the Cape, and southern right whales may be seen frequenting the outer edges of these forests, or actively manipulating a piece of floating kelp so that it rubs over the back and head. This is apparently pleasurable to the whales, and may be a way of sloughing off loose skin and parasitic whale lice.

Mating

Much boisterous playing and rolling within the breaker line by groups of up to seven or more whales may indicate mating, with several rambunctious males attempting to mate with a single female. At times, the female may not be in a co-operative mood and may flee to the shallows or lie on her back to avoid the advances of her suitors. A more detailed account of mating activities is discussed in the southern right whale section.

The Whale Trail

The South African Whale Trail has several components and covers the main route from Cape Town to Tsitsikamma in the east, the west coast whale route from Cape Town to Cape Columbine in the north, and the east coast whale route off the coast of KwaZulu-Natal. Different species of whales are distributed along our coastline and the trail is a reflection of the behavioural patterns and migratory paths of the whale species that frequent our waters. Each route has a different feel, and it depends, of course, on what you are looking for on your African sojourn. Perhaps you are here only for whales, and if this is the case, it may be worth sampling all that the different routes have to offer. If scenery and the cultures of the Cape feature high on your agenda, along with whales of course, then perhaps the southern Cape whale route is the best option. If, however, you want to take in the Big Five and then make it up to the Big Six by spotting some whales, then east coast whale watching may be the best option, as this coastline is more typically, perhaps stereotypically, African. This latter route will, however, be boat-based due to the need to access the migration routes of the humpback whales, which are heading north to their tropical breeding grounds.

Southern Cape whale route

This is South Africa's flagship whale route, which stretches from Cape Town in the west to Tsitsikamma in the east, a distance of some 650km. At the heart of the southern Cape whale route is Walker Bay, situated off the town of Hermanus. It would appear, however, that the entire coastline has been purposely made for spotting whales. If you look carefully at the morphology of this coastline and, better still, if you examine a geological map of the region, it is easy to see that the development of the major bays along the route is controlled by the geology. Stupendous tectonic forces rucked the Earth's crust into the mountains of the Cape, an event followed by 400 million years of erosion and continental rupture. The final product is the beautifully scalloped coastline, with the evocatively named False, Walker, Mossel, Plettenberg and Algoa bays. Our journey traverses these ancient rocks and it really is the combination of mountains, sky and sea that makes this coastline one of the most spectacularly beautiful in the world.

But it is not just the breathtaking beauty of this region that draws the traveller to the area. Its history is fascinating, stretching back to the age of exploration when Vasco da Gama passed this way in 1488, erecting *padrãos* (stone crosses) as punctuation marks along his route wherever he came ashore. Visiting these sites invokes a feeling of absolute isolation, way beyond the realm of the known world, braving reefs and storms, always probing into unknown territory, with dark hinterlands harbouring unknown dangers in a world governed by superstition and a wrathful God. Almost 100 years later, in 1580, Francis Drake described it as, "the fairest cape we saw in the whole circumference of the earth".

This was the age of exploration, financed by the monarchs and merchants of Europe, with one thing on their mind—loot. Without detracting from the heroic exploits of those early seafarers, the endeavours were not in any way altruistic and, to this end, South Africa, India, Batavia (modern-day Indonesia), Malaya, and the Moluccas were incorporated into the nascent European economic system; a system whose legacy still reverberates down through the centuries, and continues to manifest itself in the political and socio-economic landscape of South Africa.

Following on the voyages of those early explorers rounding the Cape and establishing a sea route to the East, Table Bay became an informal stopping place for seafarers to replenish their water supplies and gain some respite from the long months at sea. In 1652, the Dutch East India Company set up the first formal settlement and replenishing station in the shadow of Table Mountain with a view to supplying her ships with fresh supplies for the voyage east to the Moluccas, Batavia and Malaya. They had been skirmishing with the Portuguese in Angola in 1650 in an attempt to wrest the Portuguese possessions from them and, unsuccessful in this attempt, decided to establish their own station in Table Bay.

It was from this toehold on a wild and unexplored continent that expansion began—an expansion not wholly sanctioned by the Dutch East India Company. The DEIC (more properly, the VOC) were not interested in expanding the colony—wealth was being generated elsewhere, and to increase the size of the territory would be to dilute the reasons for establishing the victualling station in the first place. Human nature being as it is, however, the inexorable expansion of the colony was impossible to stop, and the outward migration of people from the Cape of Good Hope wove rich threads into the underlying tapestry of mountains, sea and sky. Nomadic farmers, explorers and wanderers pushed further and further into the hinterland and eastward along the coast. They found an immense, sparsely populated land of stunning beauty, well watered and ideal for grazing and agriculture. With time, more settlers and traders arrived, bringing wives and children, Malay slaves and freed men. Shipwrecks along the coast added other individuals to this melting pot of cultures, and when Britain occupied the Cape between 1795 and 1803 a good dose of Anglo and Celtic culture was added to the brew. Britain had taken over administration of the

Cape at the behest of William of Orange when Napoleon overran Holland during the Napoleonic Wars. Realizing that they were onto a good thing, they invaded and made it their own in 1806, beginning a phase of Anglicization of the Cape that has never entirely ended. British occupation drove a wave of emigration of Dutch settlers from the colony out into the vast African hinterland in wagons, which would lead to the colonization of the entire subcontinent.

Influences and immigration aside, the underlying bedrock of Dutch culture remained, spiced up by the influences of the Malays and Indonesians from the Dutch colonies in the East. In time, the language and culture developed its own vernacular and it is perhaps this that adds to the charm of the Cape and the Whale Trail. No one can be anything but charmed and entertained by the rich seam of culture and language that flows through the communities of Malayan descent. The Cape Dutch architecture with its Malayan influences, the white, thatched cottages of farmers and fishermen alike, the farms, smallholdings, and eventually the ordered wine estates, blend seamlessly into the rugged beauty of the natural landscape.

And then of course there are other aspects that make this one of the most unique places on Earth. Thanks to continental drift and plate tectonics, South Africa was isolated from larger Gondwana approximately 160 million years ago, which allowed for the evolution of Fynbos—the local name for the Cape Floral Kingdom. One of a total of six floral kingdoms in the world, the 6,500 species of plants exceeds that of the entire British Isles, or much of Europe for that matter. Fynbos is restricted to nutrient-poor soils and as a result grows in the sandy deposits of the Cape. Renosterveld, the other characteristic Cape vegetation, is restricted to clay soils of the southern and eastern Cape. Often confused with Fynbos, Renosterbos is the main shrub found in this type of veld. Three hundred years ago, black rhinoceros and other ungulates used to roam freely on the Renosterveld and there are those who maintain that this is how it derived its name. Others, however, believe that the vegetation's characteristic dark grey resembles that of rhinoceros hide.

In short then, this stretch of coastline has the diversity to keep any visitor fascinated for weeks. A purchase of a book on South Africa's Whale Trail would seem to indicate a leaning towards the natural world, which can be accessed in plenty along the trail. Whales, Fynbos and geology are to be found in abundance here, along with great white sharks, elephants, game reserves and birdlife. So, without further ado, let us venture forth on our whale-spotting journey and, as we travel, let us be aware of the history of the region, human and natural alike, which makes this area so infinitely fascinating on a multitude of different levels.

Whales frequent the bays of the southern Cape, and perhaps Walker Bay is the most famous of them all. However, whale densities along the coastline are variable and they vary their migratory habits over time. A 'popular' bay from a whale's point of view may fall from favour over several seasons, while other areas become more frequented. In that the whales over-winter on this coastline, prospective whale spotters must ensure that they come here during the months of May to September.

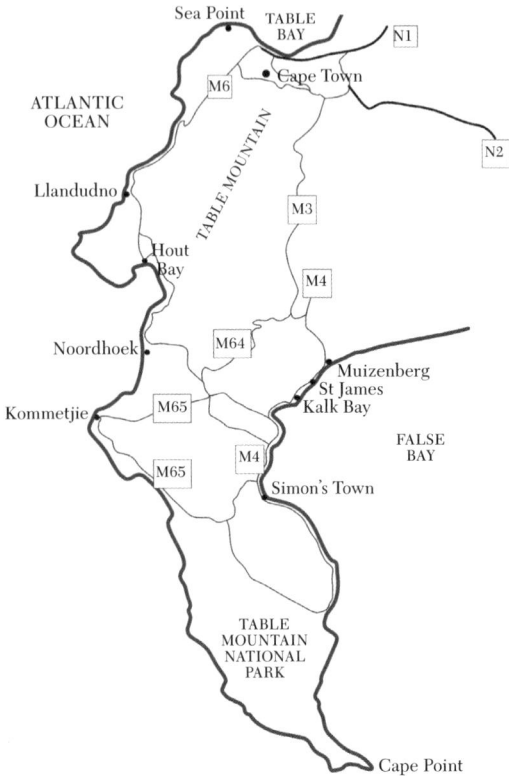

Sea Point — TABLE BAY — N1
ATLANTIC OCEAN
M6
Cape Town
TABLE MOUNTAIN
N2
Llandudno
M3
Hout Bay
M4
Noordhoek
M64
Muizenberg
St James
Kalk Bay
Kommetjie
M65
M65 — M4
FALSE BAY
Simon's Town
TABLE MOUNTAIN NATIONAL PARK
Cape Point

Cape Peninsula and False Bay

Aim to get onto the coastal road that runs from
Muizenberg to Simon's Town. Southern right whales
are often spotted along this portion of the coastline and
on the western side of the peninsula off Noordhoek,
Kommetjie, Hout Bay and Llandudno. Whale numbers
are not as high as further east, but if time is short or you
are planning on a drive around the spectacular Cape
Peninsula anyway, then there is no reason not to include
some whale watching on your sojourn. Specifically, take
the M3 southwards out of town, past the University of

Cape Town, following the signs for Muizenberg. At Lakeside, take Boyes Drive which will take you high above False Bay and the towns of St James and Kalk Bay. You are now in the best place to spot whale blows out towards the east so a pair of binoculars will be handy. If you don't see whales, the spectacular views may be compensation enough, and besides, your whale quest is not entirely over as there are still opportunities for spotting whales further along the coast. Proceeding southward, Boyes Drive will eventually take you back down to Kalk Bay. At the traffic lights, turn right and continue to head southwards until Fishhoek. Keep a weather eye out for whales in the embayment at Fishhoek as the whales often come right inshore at this spot. Pass through Fishhoek, turn left at the roundabout and continue to follow the coast southwards towards Simon's Town, still keeping those eyes open for whale blows. Beyond Simon's Town the road ascends towards Smitswinkel Bay where, once again, views out over False Bay may be had, with the chance of spotting blows or whale backs. Depending on your inclination, you can continue to follow the road, which now heads inland across the peninsula, or retrace your route back towards Fishhoek. If the return trip is opted for, then at the roundabout before Fishhoek keep left and head across the peninsula to Noordhoek and take the Chapman's Peak toll road to Hout Bay. This has to be one of the most scenic drives in the world and it is worthwhile stopping in some of the turn-outs to take in the spectacle of sea and mountains and, of course, whales if there are any in the bay. Have a look at the safety features along the route—those catch fences to check falling rocks were imported from Switzerland and installed by helicopter and rope-access crews to improve the safety of road users. Follow the signs from Hout Bay to Llandudno, via Suikerbossie Hill, following which the road descends to the sea again and then runs through to Sea Point and Cape Town. Once again there are myriad opportunities along the coast road to spot whales, so keep looking, particularly those seated on the left-hand side of the vehicle.

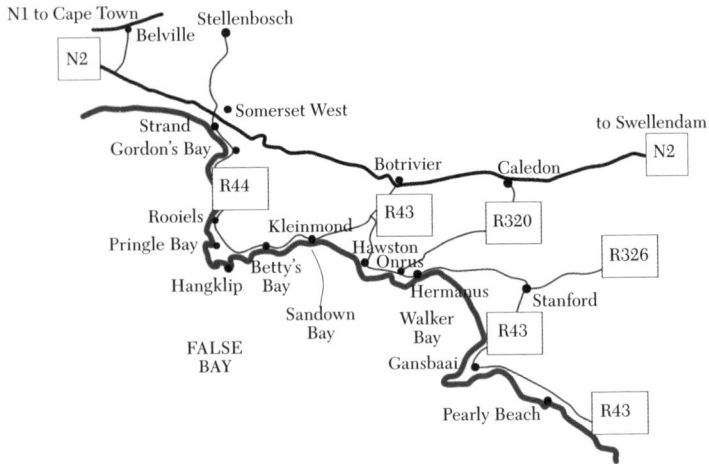

Gordon's Bay to Pearly Beach
Take the N2 eastward towards Somerset West and the Strand and then follow the signs to Gordon's Bay, which is located on the north-eastern corner of False Bay. Drive through Gordon's Bay and head south along the coast road towards Cape Hangklip and Rooi Els. Once again the road is elevated above the sea just after Gordon's Bay and there is a good chance that you will see whales on the right as you head southwards. After approximately 25km, the road swings eastward and takes you on another breathtakingly beautiful route along the coast. Opportunities of seeing whales from Cape Hangklip to Hermanus are limited, but you might get a sighting from the viewing spot in Sandown Bay where the road

comes closest to the sea. However, the spectacular drive from Cape Hangklip to Hermanus cannot be missed, so sit back, forget about whales for the moment and enjoy the drive. There is a long-defunct whaling station at Pringle Bay. Its presence indicates that whales were once prevalent along this stretch of coastline. Keep on heading east through the settlement of Kleinmond until you reach Hermanus Road. Turn right and head for the whale capital of South Africa—Hermanus. The delights of the town are well worth the stop. Beyond Hermanus the R43 takes you via Stanford to Gansbaai. Make sure to stop at De Kelders where there is great whale viewing to be had from the hotel there. If you have an interest in maritime history, it was on Danger Point that HMS *Birkenhead* struck and foundered that fateful night in 1852. Soldiers and seamen assembled on deck and held their ranks while the women and children were taken off in the boats, starting a tradition of 'women and children first', which endures to this day. Few men survived the wreck, the sharks making short work of those swimming for their lives in the cold, dark water, although not a single woman or child was drowned thanks to the gallantry and sacrifice of the soldiers and sailors.

Hermanus

The self-proclaimed capital of whale watching in South Africa, the town of Hermanus is truly the heart of the southern Cape whale trail. There is no escaping the influence of the whale in this town—it positively oozes 'whaleness'. But, why not, seeing that they have marketed themselves as the finest land-based whale watching in the world? The cliffs above Walker Bay are perfect for spotting southern

WHALE TRAIL

right whales where they come to mate, calve and avoid the hardships of a Southern Ocean winter. Hermanus is known too for its Whale Crier—the only one of his kind in the world and therefore perhaps the most threatened species on Earth. Fortunately, a hat, horn, and sandwich board, plus an extrovert personality, are all that it takes to reproduce a whale crier, although this is not to say that we shouldn't attempt to preserve our existing incumbent. During whale season, when the first whales hove into the harbour view, he strides the clifftops above Walker Bay dressed in his black trousers, white shirt and distinctive hat, keeping a weather eye out for whales. The kelp horn blasts messages over the cliffs and is carried on the keen Cape wind to the ears of eager whale watchers. There is no random blowing on the horn, mind you, but strict adherence to a local Morse code, which tells the informed listener in which bay the whales are located. For those who aren't au fait with the code, it is explained on a sandwich board, which the Whale Crier carries on him on his meanderings and pipings along the cliffs above Walker Bay. Alternatively, the local tourist office will supply you with a copy of the codes before you venture out on your quest for whales and the Crier.

Each year, there is the Hermanus Whale Festival, which celebrates the arrival of both the whales and spring. For a few days each September, Hermanus is transformed, as thousands of visitors arrive to enjoy not only the sight of whales but a variety of artistic performances. Approximately 30 shows—usually the most successful productions from South Africa's two largest art festivals—are staged each year and include the performing arts and various musical recitals. Then there are the triathlons, half marathons, cycle races and a football, or soccer, day. And if you want to have the whole Hermanus experience there is the Spring Wild Flower Festival at Fernkloof Nature Reserve, which takes place during the week prior to the Whale Festival. Visit the Old Harbour Museum where there are displays on whales and whaling paraphernalia from the days of shore-based whale hunting out of Hermanus.

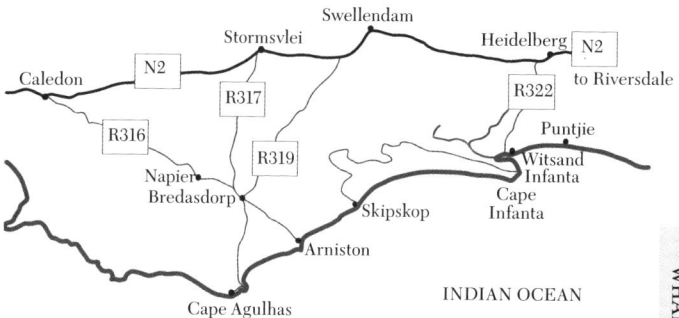

Arniston to Puntjie

Known for possibly the largest concentration of cow–calf pairs in the country, this stretch of coastline is a little inaccessible for whale watchers. There are two ways of accessing the coastline, the first being via Bredasdorp and then following the gravel road to De Hoop Nature Reserve, and the second being via Swellendam to the

Breede Rivier mouth and Cape Infanta. The distances are significant and to attempt to do both routes in a day is not a practical option. The journey begins on the N2 out of Cape Town, although if you are coming from Hermanus it is perfectly possible to jog your way across country to Bredasdorp, but be aware that you will be travelling on gravel roads and progress may be slow and at times bumpy. Assuming that you have taken the N2 option, for those opting to go to De Hoop take the Caledon turn-off and travel via Napier to Bredasdorp. In town, turn left off Long Street at the traffic light, which will take you into Lower All Saints Street. Look out for the sign 'De Hoop Nature Reserve'. Travel north-east on this road (A319) for almost 5km before turning right onto a gravel road. Travel another 33km, looking out for a right-hand turn to De Hoop Reserve. Drive another 5km, which will bring you to the entrance gate to the reserve. Once you have paid your entrance fee, head for Koppie Alleen, park your car and walk to the bluff overlooking the sea and look for whales. If you have time and are fit and organized, there is a 7km walk to Klipkoppie, where there is excellent whale viewing.

There is accommodation to be had in the reserve but this will need to be booked with CapeNature in Cape Town.

For those opting to go on to Cape Infanta and the Breede Rivier mouth, follow the N2 past Swellendam and, about 3km before Heidelberg, turn right to Port Beaufort/Witsand. The road is tarred and will take you directly to the river mouth. Where the road reaches the river, turn left and head through Witsand to the main bathing beach where good whale viewing is to be had both up and down the coast.

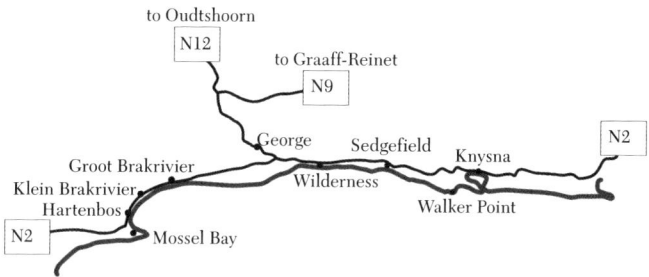

Mossel Bay to Walker Point

The best place to see whales in the town of Mossel Bay (the name of the town) is in the bay between Seal Island and Glentana. If you have a pair of binoculars, get your passengers to scan the bay as the freeway descends towards the sea. The whales tend to congregate off the river mouths, most notably at Hartenbos, Klein Brak and Groot Brak rivers. Turbidity and sediment in the water may, however, mask the presence of whales and you may need to be particularly sharp-eyed to spot the creatures. Focus on the last line of breakers from the beach as this is where they usually congregate.

Travelling further eastward past the town of George, the road enters the Touws Rivier gorge just before The Wilderness. Attend to the bends here, for they are incredibly tight, and if they don't get you the speed cameras will. On the final bend before the descent to The Wilderness, is Dolphin Point and, as the name implies, it is worth making a stop here to see if there are any dolphins about, and if you are lucky, perhaps even whales. Again, be careful of traffic when entering and exiting the parking and viewing area.

Walker Point to Nature's Valley

Along this stretch of coastline, southern right whales favour the bay at Plettenberg Bay, particularly between Lookout Beach and the Keurbooms Rivier. Land-based viewing is not at its optimum, although one may see blows from Beacon Island, the top of Signal Hill or from the Robbeberg Peninsula. Good views can be obtained from the beach at the Keurbooms Rivier mouth if the whales are in a co-operative frame of mind. Generally, whales in this region are not accompanied by calves and hence stay out in the slightly deeper water, which makes land-based watching somewhat more difficult, so a boat trip is probably the best way of seeing them.

Moving slightly eastward, you may find cow–calf pairs in the vicinity of Nature's Valley, situated approximately 20km east of Plettenberg Bay. Follow the signs from the N2, and travel down the winding Grootrivierspas to the river at the bottom valley floor. It is a marvellous drive through thick coastal forest, and the soft green light filtering through the overhead canopy is a wonderful contrast to the often harsh light of the seascapes we have been encountering so far. Follow the signs to Nature's Valley, drive through the settlement, find somewhere to park and then take the 2km walk to the cliff edge at the mouth of the Sout Rivier. Sightings of southern rights are possible here, although there is more chance of spotting humpback or bottlenose dolphins in the surf zone.

This then is essentially the end of the southern Cape whale route. Travelling eastward and north-east,

Southbound Pocket Guides

numbers of southern right whales decrease significantly. However, further offshore the humpback whales may be seen on their annual migrations to tropical seas and it is out of the ports of Durban and Richards Bay on the east coast that these whales may be spotted. Sperm whales are also known to frequent our coastline, although little is known about their migratory habits. A narrow continental shelf and deep water off the Eastern Cape in the vicinity of Port St Johns allows sperm whales to come close inshore but the frequency of their visits is currently not known.

Other southern Cape attractions

There is a plethora of things to interest even the most jaded traveller along the Whale Trail. There are whales, of course, and then there is Cape Town and all the quaint towns along the route. There are restaurants aplenty, Cape culture too, touristy spots and downright ugly spots, and this guide cannot hope to cover every aspect and attraction of this long coastline. All this guide can aspire to is to point you in the direction of some of the best experiences to be had along the Whale Trail.

Cape Town is a world of its own, with attractions both varied and bewildering in their scope. Art, culture, beautiful scenery, beaches, restaurants and universities are all part of the scene, all of which are overshadowed by the brooding presence of the mountain. In keeping with the sea-life theme, visit the Two Oceans Aquarium at the Cape Town Waterfront. The main tank is a feat of engineering in itself, and one feels almost underwater when standing up against the seamless glass sides and peering into the dark kelp forests that grow so happily in the captive world of Aquariana. The rest of the Waterfront is also a must-see, undeniably the most frequented tourist spot in South Africa. It is easy to see why, with its easy-going atmosphere, old world feel, the bustle of a real working harbour and the backdrop of Table Mountain. Take the boat from here to Robben Island (a World Heritage Site), where a number of PAC and ANC activists, including its most famous incumbent, Nelson Mandela, were incarcerated for a number of years.

Another famous attraction of Cape Town is the wine estates. It has been said that they are the most beautiful in the world and should be visited as part of any grand tour of the province. Gracious country estates, some of them dating back to the early days of the colony, set amongst oak trees, and vineyards with mountain backdrops are experiences that should not to be missed. Then there are the wines for which the Cape is famous, and which have been gracing the tables of Europe for 300 years. There are wine estates at the back of the mountain in Constantia, a host around Stellenbosch and Durbanville, as well as out towards Paarl, Worcester and Robertson.

False Bay and the coastline out towards Hermanus is world famous for its great white sharks—bringing in film crews and photographers, such as David Doubillet, the well-known *National Geographic* underwater photographer. Shark diving and whale watching can also be had off Dyer Island, with cruises run by an operator of the same name. The trips start from the Kleinbaai harbour, which lies to the east of Danger Point of HMS *Birkenhead* fame. The trip heads towards Pearly Beach, where one of the highest concentrations of southern right whales along this coastline occurs, season dependent of course. After spending the allotted time with these magnificent creatures, the tour proceeds on towards Dyer Island which is renowned for its African penguins as well as various other seabirds. Beyond Dyer Island is Geyser Rock, which is home to about 60,000 Cape fur seals, and between these two islands is Shark

Alley, world renowned for its great white sharks. This is probably the only trip on Earth where there is a good chance of seeing both southern right whales and great white sharks.

A number of wonderful reserves managed by CapeNature are located around Cape Town and the Whale Trail, the details of which are given in the contacts section at the back. The most obvious reserve to visit when in Cape Town is the Cape Point Nature Reserve on the southern tip of the Cape Peninsula. It is widely believed that this marks the point where the Atlantic and Indian oceans meet, but this is in fact incorrect—the actual places lies some 160km to the east at Cape Agulhas, which is the southernmost point of Africa. Take the funicular up to the lookout and enjoy the views out over False Bay to the east and the wider Atlantic to the west.

Much of Table Mountain is reserve area too, and there are many walks and climbs up, over, and around the mountain, which are open to all, and suitable for all levels of walking ability. Travelling eastward, and particularly applicable to whale watchers, is De Hoop Nature Reserve. It was once a military missile-testing area, which in a way was its saving grace. Its whale-watching benefits have already been described, but it has other attractions within its 34,000 hectares of Cape Floral Kingdom fynbos. The reserve also stretches three nautical miles out to sea, offering protection to all marine life within this zone. Hiking, cycling and birdwatching are added attractions to the whale watching to be had on the rocky outcrops of the reserve. It is an important conservation area for lowland fynbos, providing the largest area for this vegetation type. The Bredasdorp/Agulhas and Infanta areas provide habitat for 1,500 plant species of the approximately 9,000 species found in the Cape Floristic Region. The reserve also boasts

WHALE TRAIL

86 mammal species, including the rare bontebok, Cape mountain zebra, eland, grey rhebok, baboon, mongoose, caracal and leopard. In addition, the reserve is noted for its resident and migratory bird life, with more than 260 species having been recorded in the reserve, including the endangered Cape vulture.

The surrounding towns have their own attractions too—Stellenbosch with its ancient oak trees and traditional Dutch architecture; Paarl with her fantastic pearl of granite and mountains; Worcester hinting at the great Karoo, and the African hinterland beyond. All are steeped in original Dutch settler and Malay culture and are the richer for it. Moving out eastward along the coast there are myriad towns—Caledon, Bredasdorp, Riviersonderend, Swellendam, Heidelberg, Riversdale, Mossel Bay, George, Knysna, Wilderness, Plettenberg Bay—a list which does little to enlighten but hints at immense possibilities, nonetheless. The larger centres of Swellendam, Mossel Bay, George, Knysna and Plettenberg Bay are delightful towns with histories that reflect the lives of the original settlers and the hardships, wars, triumphs and failures of a self-reliant people.

Arniston is worth a stop—charming, white-washed fishermen's cottages dot the cliffs above the sea, drawing tourists and artists alike who come to look and paint as is their wont. Swellendam, once a far-flung outpost of the colony, nestles in graceful charm at the foot of the mountains, secure in her 260-year-old history and her stern, Cape Dutch buildings. Visit the water mill and Ambagswerf for insights into the life of the original burghers and farmers of the district. Mossel Bay is a major centre and the home of South Africa's natural gas facility—a mini Aberdeen of the south. There is the old Post Office Tree and museum to visit, commemorating the voyages of Vasco da Gama in 1488. Mossel Bay has made the symbol of the *padrão* their own. The *padrão* is a stone cross erected on headlands overlooking the sea, which marked high or turning points in their voyages. George and Knysna are charming, and the sights, history and entertainment along this portion of what is known as the Garden Route are outstanding. Freshly grown oysters straight out of the lagoon, washed down with chilled champagne, are to be had on and around the lagoon, while drives over the Phantom Pass and train rides on the Outeniqua Choo Choo are all mandatory experiences. The local tourist offices will be able to provide details on what to see and do. Plettenberg Bay is the next stop, and where Knysna and George are more genteel, 'Plett', as it is known to the locals, has a slightly more modern, brash air. Grand scenery, good whale watching and some excellent restaurants keep it firmly embedded in the tourist route itinerary. Beyond the town and the Keurbooms River is an area known as the Crags, which is also home to some other interesting experiences. The Elephant Sanctuary, Birds of Eden and Monkey Land are located here, and all three institutions provide homes to traumatized, lost, abandoned animals, but in the most amazing environments. The dome that covers the bird enclosure is larger than London's Millennium Dome, and the Monkey Land enclosure is of similar proportions. Different species of birds and primates from all over the world cohabitate in apparent harmony within the confines of their new home. The Elephant Sanctuary similarly provides homes to several African elephants that have been rescued from difficult circumstances, and a visit to this park will reward you with close encounters of a pachyderm kind. Further east, is the Tsitsikamma Reserve, which is a wonderful forest area adjacent to the ocean. The first forest canopy tour in South Africa was set up here and is well worth the experience. For the more sedate there are walks to be had in the reserve and along the rugged coastline with its inlets and wonderful suspension bridge. There is even a snorkelling trail within the embayments of the reserve.

If the coastline loses its appeal, or a sense of curiosity brings on a need to see what is beyond the mountains, then follow these compulsions, for beyond those mountains is another world—a world incredibly different from the relatively lush coastline. For a start, the journey over the passes is spectacular, especially when you consider that the passes have their origins 400 million years back in time and are but a remnant of their original size. Descending to the plains below, the traveller will be struck by the harshness of the light, the rugged grandeur of the scenery and the paucity of vegetation. This is the Klein Karoo, a semi desert in the rain shadow of the mountains. It is also sheep and ostrich country, farming pursuits which strangely enough seem to do well here. The Karoo has almost mythical status in the collective psychology of South Africa, which is perhaps due to the vastness of the terrain, the aridity of the land, and the looming presence of mountains and flat-topped koppies. Visit the towns of Montagu and Oudtshoorn and be sure to visit the Cango Caves north of Oudtshoorn—a wonderland of stalactites and stalagmites to rival any similar grotto elsewhere. The drive over the Swartberg Pass is a must—the scenery is breathtaking and the horizons go on forever—but allow some time for the journey, as the road is untarred and the hairpins tight. At Prince Albert have a snoop around the town before heading back to Oudtshoorn via Meiring's Poort—a narrow defile which cuts right through the very heart of the mountain range.

Top: Humpback whale lobtailing.

Above: Dusk settles on False Bay.

CAPE TO CAIRO

the KALK BAY GALLERY

Above: Evening settles on Kalk Bay, on the Cape's pristine peninsula.

Left and far left: The streets of Kalk Bay are lined with quaint galleries and antique shops, with restaurants and coffee shops tucked in alleyways.

Top: Tidal pools on the southern Cape peninsula.
Above: Southern right whale mother and calf.

Kalk Bay harbour.

Top: Colonial hotel in Simon's Town.
Above: Simon's Town boardwalk is reminiscent of the Cape Colony of yesteryear.
Right: Lighthouse in the Simon's Town harbour.

Top: The coastline at the De Hoop Nature Reserve.
Above: De Hoop boardwalk.

Top: Hiking in the De Hoop Nature Reserve.
Above: Whale watching off the cliffs of De Hoop.

Top: Cliffs of Hermanus, one of the most popular whale watching spots on the southern Cape coast.
Above: Old Hermanus harbour.
Right: Boat charters from Hermaus.

SOUTHERN RIGHT CHARTERS
082 353 0550

THE WHALE SHACK

BOOKING OF
BOAT TRIPS D

NEXT TRIP

Left: Marimba player in Hermanus.
Top: The Marine, Hermanus.
Centre: The Whaler, Hermanus.
Above: Whale weather vane in Hermanus.

Top: Walker Bay.
Above: Sidewalk cafés in Hermanus.

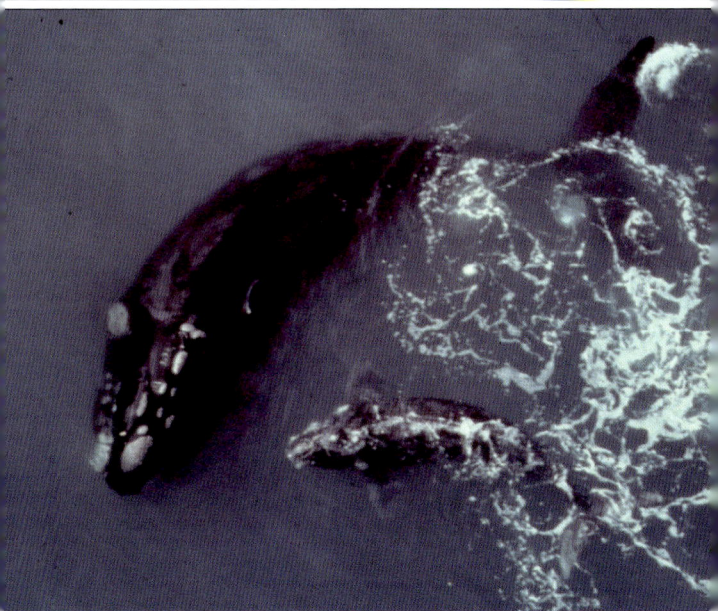

Southern right whale mother and calf in Walker Bay.

Top: Skeleton of a blue whale mounted at the South African Museum in Cape Town.

Above: War memorial in Heramus.

West coast whale route

WHALE TRAIL

West coast whale route

Heading north out of Cape Town is the west coast whale route, a region that boasts a high occurrence of whales along its coastline. The west coast route is quite different to the southern route, comprising vast stretches of wild open space, Fynbos, lonely windswept beaches and a stark beauty, which differs immensely from the mountainous scenery of the southern coastline. Access to the coast and the whales is difficult due to the West Coast Road (R27) being set some distance from the sea, with few side roads providing access to the beach.

Melkbosstrand to Cape Columbine

Approximately 20km north of Cape Town, it is worth taking the road to Melkbosstrand, as cow–calf pairs do occasionally frequent the bay here. Search as far as Ou Skip before returning to the R27 and proceeding north. Southern rights may also be seen in the bay at Yzerfontein, where there are some low promontories, which are useful for getting a view of the ocean. The turnoff for Yzerfontein is approximately 70km out of Cape Town, following which it is an 8km ride down to the coast. Further north, whales congregate between Langebaan Lagoon and Vondeling Island, but unfortunately the only accessible viewing spot is at Plankiesbaai, immediately to the north of Vondeling Island. Another obstacle is the fact that this lies within the West Coast National Park with access limited to the months of August and September when the wild flowers are in full bloom. This does correspond with the whale season, but one needs to synchronize one's visit with the flowers, which can of course be rather unpredictable.

To get there, take the left-hand turn-off from the R27 signposted 'Churchhaven' and 'Park', located approximately 14km past the Yzerfontein turn-off. Only partially tarred, the road traverses sand/veld, then follows the peninsula between the lagoon and the sea. Approximately 25km after entering the park, take the turn-off to Plankiesbaai on your left and follow the track to the sea where there is a parking area and a picnic spot. A high knoll to the south of the parking area is worth the climb, providing good viewing of Vondeling Island, the sea and, if you are lucky, some whales.

Cape Columbine to Lambert's Bay

St Helena Bay, which is defined by Cape Columbine in the south and Lambert's Bay in the north, was an important whaling ground for southern right whales during the early nineteenth century. Populations are again increasing to the extent that the bay may become one of the more important nodes of right whales along the South African coast. The whales congregate just offshore of Die Vlei (Rocher Pan), approximately 10km north of Dwarskersbos. This area is located a fair distance from the R27, but if you feel a little adventurous, follow the R27 to the bridge at the Berg River crossing at Laaiplek/ Velddrif, After the bridge, turn left at the T-junction and follow the signs to Laaiplek and to the road running north marked Dwarskersbos. After passing through Dwarskersbos the dirt road turns inland at the southern end of Die Vlei. Approximately 12km past Dwarskersbos is the entrance gate to the Rocher Pan Nature Reserve (opening times 08h00 to 17h00 to 31 August, 07h00 to 18h00 thereafter). Once within the reserve, find your way to the pan and then walk 50m from the parking area next to the pan to the beach and once again, hopefully, there will be some whales in the bay, particularly after the fairly long drive to get here. If not, content yourself with the abundance of bird life that resides in the pan.

WHALE TRAIL

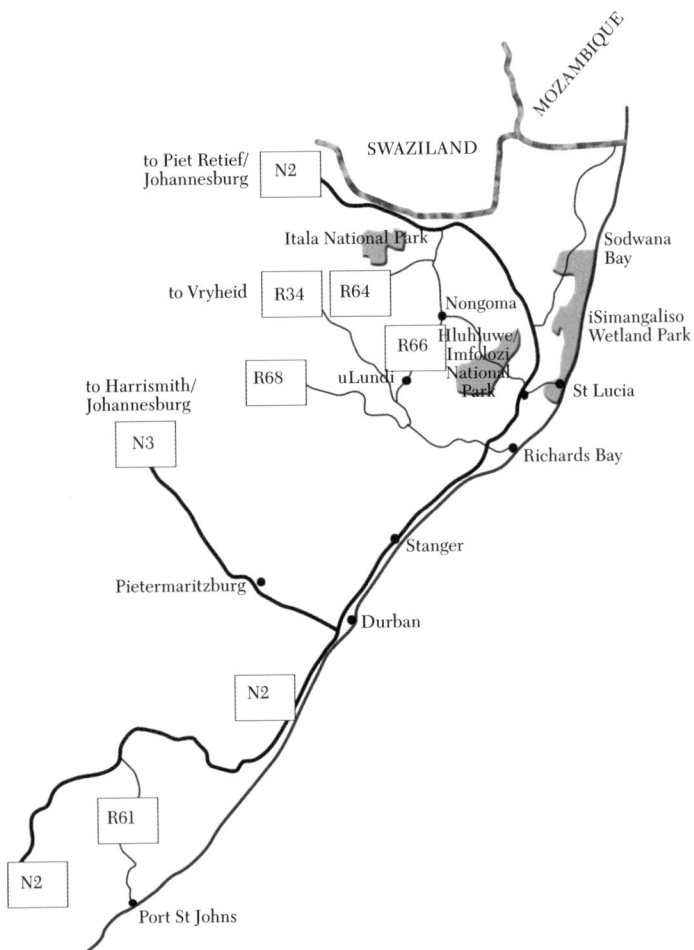

to Piet Retief/
Johannesburg

MOZAMBIQUE

SWAZILAND

N2

Itala National Park

Sodwana
Bay

to Vryheid

R34

R64

Nongoma

iSimangaliso
Wetland Park

R66

Hluhluwe/
Imfolozi
National
Park

to Harrismith/
Johannesburg

R68

uLundi

St Lucia

N3

Richards Bay

Stanger

Pietermaritzburg

Durban

N2

R61

N2

Port St Johns

The east coast whale route

Whaling has taken place along the east coast since the late seventeenth century, most notably out of the port of Durban. As a youngster, I can remember seeing whales tied up at the slipway adjacent to the whaling station, before their last journey into the processing factory. These were humpback whales, which were taken on their annual migration northwards to tropical seas, as well as Bryde's, blue, fin and sei whales—all rorquals in fact. Back then, it all seemed quite the norm, and family friends who worked within the industry used to bring us sperm whale teeth and slabs of frozen whale meat, but I shudder at the thought today. All those old whalers are long retired or have since passed away, but their legacy to some extent lives on in the depleted whale populations along our coast.

The east coast has an entirely different feel to it when compared to the Cape. It is more 'African', perhaps, if you are one for stereotypes. Rolling hills, deeply incised rivers, and red earth characterize the landscape. Thorn trees and euphorbia punctuate the savannah and provide shade for numerous traditional homesteads. The huge embayments are gone; replaced by a dune-fringed coastline cut by languid estuaries and lagoons with associated mangrove swamps, bird and animal life. These estuaries in their heyday were havens for fish, hippopotami, crocodiles and birdlife, and in a number of places are still relatively unspoilt. Hippos and crocodiles are long gone from these lagoons, although in Richards Bay there is no shortage of crocodiles, and in iSimangaliso (St Lucia) Wetland Park there is no shortage of hippopotami either. Seas are subtropical and hence warmer, which of course attracts a different kind of sea life. Dolphins proliferate along this coastline and it is a common sight to see them surfing the breakers or breaching in vast schools on the open sea. Due to the warmer water, conditions are more favourable for corals and reef life, and diving doesn't require the same thicknesses of neoprene as the Cape. The east coast's two core diving centres are Umkomaas and Sodwana Bay, each with their particular attractions. Every July, there is the annual sardine run, when countless millions of sardines migrate northwards along the coastline. This is bonanza time for animals and fishermen alike, as gamefish, sharks, dolphins and birds follow the shoals, gorging themselves on nature's bounty. Diving during the sardine run can be a heady and somewhat adrenaline-pumping experience. Another aquatic attraction is the ragged-toothed sharks, which migrate to Aliwal Shoal during the winter months to breed. In short, the winter months are boom time for the east coast. Temperatures are perfect, the seas relatively warm, the rains have stopped, and once the scene is set, the actors on life's great stage make their entrance—whales, sharks and sardines to provide one of the greatest shows on Earth, or as the sardine run advocates would say, 'the greatest shoal on Earth'.

Humpback whales are the flagship species for the east coast whale route, although blue, fin, sei and Bryde's whales also occur along this coastline. All these whales were taken by the whaling station at Durban during its operational years. An occasional vanguard of humpbacks arrives in April, but the real season is May to November, with a few stragglers bringing up the rear as late as January. A few pairs of southern right whales also manage to make it this far north every year, along with an occasional minke whale. Humpback whale numbers are recovering and each year more and more whales are recorded. Three migration routes seem to be followed by the whales up the east coast of Africa to their breeding grounds. The first route is defined by a landfall in the vicinity of Knysna, following which the whales work their way up the coast to central Mozambique. The second is straight through the Mozambique Channel and on to the Comoros, and the third heads directly for southern Madagascar. Apparently these three population groups are quite distinct, to the extent that they have even developed their own songs. There does appear to be some crossover between the groups on the odd occasion. Northward migration brings on a display of breaching and singing amongst the male members of the population, which is worth trying to see. Mid to late July sees the start of the slower, southward journey back towards the Antarctic waters and is generally more sedate and closer inshore due to the mothers having new calves.

Durban

Durban has had a long, and at times fractious, relationship with whales, but now the only boats that venture forth from Durban Harbour are Ocean Safaris, with the sole intention of taking tourists on dolphin and sea-life charters, with the added bonus of possibly encountering whales on the trip. They have an 80 percent whale-spotting success rate in terms of spotting whales from June to November. Their safari covers all the various aspects of marine and mammal life in the sea immediately around Durban. This includes the shark net system, fish life, real-time footage of reef life from their wet camera and, of course, an excellent chance of seeing whales during the season. If conditions are good, there may even be opportunities for snorkelling over some of the reefs.

There are four departures each day from uShaka Marine World, weather depending, and the trip generally lasts from 45 minutes to one hour. In addition, they organize dive charters in Mozambique, Sodwana Bay, Durban, Aliwal Shoal and Protea Banks should there be a strong urge to get into the water.

St Lucia

The only whale-watching permit in KwaZulu-Natal is held by Advantage Charters, which operates out of the town of St Lucia in Northern KwaZulu-Natal—gateway to the iSimangaliso Park. ISimangaliso is a World Heritage Site and it is worth the trip north to experience what the region has to offer—some of South Africa's flagship game parks, the world-renowned Hluhluwe-Imfolozi parks, which were pivotal in the preservation of the black and white rhino, the extraordinary wetland areas of iSimangaliso (St Lucia), turtle breeding grounds and the whales.

Advantage Charters operates a 9m hard-hulled vessel to take whale watchers out to the migration routes. In addition to the whales, there will be an abundance of bird life, dolphins, turtles in season, sharks and, if luck holds, whale sharks and marlin. And, if the sea gods are really smiling, there is the chance of seeing a 40-ton humpback breaching a mere 50 metres from the boat. They also lower a hydrophone into the water to listen to the whale songs, which is an experience in itself.

The tour takes approximately three hours, divided into two hours on the ocean, and half an hour either side of this to travel to and from the launch site.

Shore-based whale watching

Shore-based whale watching is possible, but the whales are usually in excess of 3km offshore, although they do tend to come closer inshore on their return southwards. Port St Johns and the Transkei (Eastern Cape) coasts have great high cliffs, which serve as grand viewpoints for whale watching should there be some whales fairly close inshore.

The greatest shoal on Earth

The annual sardine run, which takes place along the

Transkei and KwaZulu-Natal South Coast, has been dubbed 'the greatest shoal on Earth'. The run, or migration, of sardines begins off the Agulhas Banks in the cold Cape waters, where tens of thousands of fish form up into hundreds of swirling shoals. Current thinking is that incursions of cold water from the Agulhas Banks creep up the southern coast of KwaZulu-Natal during the winter months. This incursion of cold water somehow seems to encourage the sardine shoals to embark on a long, lemming-like dash to nowhere. The shoals can reach lengths of 15km (10 miles), widths of 3km (two miles) and depths of nearly 40m (120ft). With this much protein heading north, it is not surprising to find that the shoals are followed by literally thousands of predators, gorging themselves at the banquet of the year. It has been estimated that in excess of 20,000 dolphins follow the shoals, along with countless sharks, as well as seals and orcas. From the air, tens of thousands of cormorants and Cape gannets harass the shoals with their efficient dive-bombing manoeuvres. Payback time comes once the shoals are past though, as it is a long flight back to their usual hunting grounds, and a bout of bad weather can strand exhausted birds on the beaches. The arrival of the common dolphin appears to herald the arrival of the sardine run, and the females may in fact use the additional protein source to assist them in weaning their calves and to replenish depleted fat reserves. The dolphin pods form hunting lines just below the surface that stretch for over a kilometre or more, and when the signal goes out the entire pod will turn and force a portion of the shoal to the surface where the dolphins can hunt and breathe more easily. Once the shoals are on the surface, the seabirds pile in for the feast. Cape fur seals, game fish and sharks add to the list of self-invited guests feasting at the annual party. In 2002, an orca made an appearance at the sardine run, perfectly timed to coincide with a National Geographic film crew who had come over to film the spectacle.

Occasionally the shoals will beach themselves, allowing them to be netted or just scooped out of the water with buckets or any handy receptacle. During the migration, the Natal Sharks Board lifts the shark nets, emplaced to protect the bathing beaches, to allow the free passage of fish and predators alike.

There are three ways of getting to grips with the sardine run, which occurs between May and July every year. Option 1, and certainly the simplest, is to grab binoculars and head for the KwaZulu-Natal South Coast and view the show from the following vantage points, listed from south to north:

o Splash Rocks—Port Edward
o Leisure Bay
o Walkway between Kidds Beach and Glenmore Beach
o The Head—Southbroom
o The Pier—Margate
o Lilliecrona Boulevard—between Margate and Uvongo
o Saint's Walk—between Uvongo and St Michaels-on-Sea
o Shelly Beach
o The Lighthouse—Port Shepstone
o The Lookout—Hibberdene
o Ifafa Beach
o Rocky Bay
o Scottburgh
o Warner Beach

There is a sardine hotline number, which provides updates on the location of the shoals and other information pertinent to the event.

When whale and sardine spotting, exercise some caution as large wave sets have been known to wash people off the rocks. Should the shoals come inshore, be aware that two types of predator may be in the shallow water—sharks and human—and the distinction between predator and prey in the shallows may become very blurred. The lookout spots are also good vantage points for observing the migrating whales further out to sea.

The second option is to take a cruise aboard a charter boat, which will take you into the centre of the mêlée of dolphins, sharks, seals, whales and game fish. The Natal Sharks Board runs a two-hour trip out of Durban harbour, but there are numerous operators along the coast who run similar trips.

Thirdly, and perhaps most glamorously, strap yourself into a microlight and fly over the teeming ocean to take in the sights of millions of sardines and predators in a frenzy of flight and pursuit.

Other attractions of the east coast

In keeping with the sea life theme, a visit to the Natal Sharks Board is a must. For over 40 years, this institution has been placing, maintaining and lifting shark nets along the KwaZulu-Natal coastline, making them safe for swimmers and surfers. Since 1964, there have been only two shark attacks along protected beaches, compared to several in the years preceding, culminating in the summer of 1957–58 when there were five deaths due to shark attacks, occurring over a 107-day period known as Black December.

However, it is not all about preventing shark attacks, and the Sharks Board carries out world-class research on shark behaviour and on more eco-friendly ways of combating shark attacks. They consult globally and have been leaders in changing public attitudes to sharks. They are based on Umhlanga Ridge, just to the north of Durban, and conduct public presentations and audio-visual displays on their work and sharks in general. They also run their charter boat out of Durban harbour, which is well worth the trip for nothing more than to marvel at the skill and knowledge of the skippers who host the trips.

For those who want to dive this coastline, there are a number of operators between Park Rynie and Sodwana Bay, and their contact details are included in the contacts section. Similarly for the fishing and yacht charters and shark diving. Then there are the land-based pursuits— perhaps a visit to the uShaka Marine World is a good way of making the transition from sea to land. Massive tanks house most of the fish and shark species that occur along this coastline, and the sunken-ship theme is great fun, especially for the kids.

Inland from the coast, there is a veritable feast of activities. KwaZulu-Natal boasts two of South Africa's World Heritage Sites which are both musts on any travel agenda—uKhahlamba (Drakensberg) and iSimangaliso (St Lucia) wetland area. High mountains, the possibility of snow in the winter, the second-richest heritage of cave art on Earth, and the highest pub in Africa are but a brief overview of what uKhahlamba has to offer. Isimangaliso, on the other hand, is a massive lake and estuarine system, which is home to crocodiles, hippos, elephants and abundant bird life. Its geological history is also fascinating—a record of high sea levels and abundant ammonites before all, including the dinosaurs, were extinguished by a massive meteorite impact at the end of the Cretaceous.

Pietermaritzburg, approximately 80km inland from Durban, boasts some of the finest examples of colonial Victorian architecture in the world, although the local authorities seem little interested in preserving this heritage. Further inland, there are the battlefields where much of the violent history that still haunts South Africa was enacted. Battles between British troops and Boer burghers over land, gold and diamonds were fought at Spioenkop, Ladysmith, Colenso and Talana during the Anglo–Boer War, which was fought between 1899 and 1902. Other battlefields of an even earlier war are also to be found in the sun-drenched hinterland, with the immortal names of Isandhlwana and Rorke's Drift. This was a war between Britain and the Zulus, fighting once again over control of land and resources.

Travelling north of the Thukela River, one enters the kingdom of the Zulus—perhaps the most famous of any African people. Courage, endurance, and absolute ruthlessness in combat welded the disparate tribes into a single kingdom, which dominated the political landscape of south-eastern Africa. The Zulu superpower reigned until its clash with another empire, but one with a global reach and massive resources at its disposal—Britain. The Zulu legions, or impis, ultimately met defeat at the hands of troops armed with technologically superior weapons, greater resources, but no less brave soldiers. Zulu culture is everywhere, and it is recommended that visitors to this province take in the Shakaland experience. It is also worth visiting Dingaanstad and the site of one of the early royal kraals at Gingindlovu. Township tours are also available, and provide insights into South Africa's, more recent, apartheid past.

Mahatma Gandhi spent over 20 years in South Africa and it was at his Phoenix settlement north of Durban that he developed many of his ideas, which eventually led to British withdrawal from India. The Phoenix settlement and his original printing press may be visited as part of the Inanda Heritage route. Gandhi lived within the local Indian community, which has since grown to be the largest Indian community outside of India. Their contribution to South Africa's culture is enormous, in terms of their food, architecture, music, religion, literature and intellectual capital. And on the topic of Indian cuisine, don't leave Durban without trying a local classic—'bunny-chow'—which comprises curry in a hollowed-out quarter loaf of bread.

KwaZulu-Natal Ezemvelo Wildlife is the custodian of the province's wilderness areas, and trips to Hluhluwe-Imfolozi, Tala, iSimangaliso, and Ndumo reserves are a must for game viewing. Hluhluwe-Imfolozi has the Big Five, but this in no way detracts from the other reserves. Ndumo is a bird-watcher's paradise and worth the drive to the far north of the province.

Of whales and men

Whales and men have had a long, and at times fractious, relationship. Their sheer size cannot but impress itself on any observer, whether confined to the land or voyaging on the open sea. Whales, and their smaller cousins, dolphins, have featured large in numerous myths of the ancients—influences that echo down the centuries to the modern day. The constellation Delphinus was, according to Hellenic mythology, placed in the sky by Poseidon after a dolphin assisted him in finding his future bride, Amphitrite, in a grotto beneath the waves. It is in a way a projection by the ancients of the significance of these sea creatures into the heavens, intimating a sense of unity between oceans, sky and humanity. Dolphins were the escorts of Aphrodite, Atargatis and Eros, and the salvation of Arion. Western civilization is the inheritor of much of Greek and Roman culture, and their myths add to the rich tapestry of our lives. Homer's Hymn to Apollo describes how the temple at Delphi was founded by Apollo after a journey that had taken him all over Greece in the quest for a suitable temple site. He eventually chose a lonely cave at the foot of Mount Parnassos and then, in the guise of a dolphin, he commandeered a Cretan ship and directed the winds to blow them around the coast into the harbour below the cave. His hostages were then instructed to live in the new temple and serve him as priests, praying to him as Apollo Delphinus.

Dolphins featured in art and sculpture throughout the Levant, Mesopotamia and more latterly throughout the Roman Empire. Petra, located many miles from the sea in the Jordanian desert, boasts a carving of a dolphin. It is the dolphin that carries souls to the Island of the Blest in Roman literature, and in this light featured prominently in their art and literature. Effigies of dolphins have been found in the hands of the dead in the region around the Black Sea, and taken together point to the dolphins as having an important role in the rhythms of life and death and the journey to the afterlife. Perhaps the water realm was seen to embody all that was terrible and dead, but dolphins had managed to overcome the barrier between the breathing, living world and the watery wastes below. We have read of the story of Arion, the musician, who was forced to leap overboard by his treacherous crew and was rescued by a dolphin who carried him to safety and facilitated the ultimate thwarting of his would-be murderers. The recurring stories of dolphins rescuing sailors are prominent in myth and folklore. Dolphins have been set above other animals not only because they are friendly to humans, but because they have a sense of morality and honour. "Diviner than a dolphin is nothing yet created," wrote the Greek poet, Oppian.

In some myths, whales and dolphins are connected with birth and the womb, while in others they are the conveyers of the dead. Jonah and the whale features large in Christian thinking—the saviour whale being a vanguard of a recurring Biblical saviour and redemption theme, which reaches its apogee in the New Testament. Other Biblical stories describe how the first creature God released into the waters was the whale: "And God said, 'Let the waters bring forth abundantly the moving creature that have life' ... And God created the great whales, and every living creature that moveth." The quintessential Biblical whale is the enormous Leviathan—a symbol of evil, focal point of all human fears and the embodiment of unmitigated power that God created on the fifth day of Creation as a warning to mankind.

But other influences abound, from *Tales from the Arabian Nights,* where Sinbad the sailor came ashore on an island, only to find that it was actually a giant

Accommodation in De Hoop Nature Reserve:

Top left: Cupidos Kraal.

Centre left: Potberg.

Below: Vaalkrans hut.

De Hoop Nature Reserve

Robbeberg peninsula,
Plettenberg Bay

Top left and right: Contrasting landscapes of the De Hoop Nature Reserve.
Below left: Inland in the Reserve.

Elephant rides at the Elephant Sanctuary in Plettenberg Bay.

Top left: Birds of Eden walkway.
Centre left: Blue front Amazon parrot at Birds of Eden.
Below left: Toucan.
Above: Cliffs of Gearing Point, Walker Bay.

Top: Sunset over Plettenberg Bay.

Far left: Guided boat trips in Plettenberg Bay.

Left: The Plettenberg offers luxury accommodation for its guests.

Above: Dolphin sculpture in the village.

Monkeyland Primate Sanctuary, Plettenberg Bay:

Top: White-handed gibbon.

Right: Ring-tailed lemur.

Left: Swing bridge at the sanctuary offers visitors a good view of the treetops.

Top left: Humpback whale, St Lucia. (*Danie Bennet*)
Centre left: Whaleshark. (*Colin Ogden*)
Below right: Sodwana Bay beach.
Top right: Bottlenose dolphin, Elephant Coast. (*Colin Ogden*)
Above: St Lucia village.

Top: Orca breaching.
Below: Orca spy-hopping.

whale, to Pinocchio's father who was swallowed by a whale in the beloved children's story. In Inuit or Eskimo mythology, Sedna was the goddess of the sea and the whale was her most magnificent subject. However, she also knew her own mind and married a bird in spite of the overtures of a host of suitors. Outraged by her actions, her father killed her bird husband and carried her home in a boat. For some unknown reason, he then threw her overboard, but she clung desperately to the sides of the vessel, which led him to chop off her fingers, one by one, until she fell back into the water. She then turned into the huge, voracious deity of the Lower World and ruled over all the creatures that dwelt in the sea, while each of her severed fingers turned into a different animal, amongst others a right whale, a narwhal, a beluga and a seal.

To the ancients, myths served as interpretations of natural phenomena, and as humankind has changed through time, so have the subjects of our mythology. But in spite of the change, echoes of the myths still reverberate down through the centuries. Science and the information age may have brought us rational knowledge of our world, but this may possibly be forgotten during a whale encounter, as the observer is overawed by the bulk and beauty of the beast. How does one explain such an experience without resorting to the language of allegory and metaphor? It is easy to see how such an encounter can become embellished into myth, particularly in the world of the ancients where rational thought, communication and the dissemination of information were very different from today's. Seafarers are naturally superstitious, the superstition being a legacy of thousands of years of venturing forth into a wild, unpredictable and dangerous world. Despite our modern technology, the unpredictability of the watery realm persists, but to frightened impressionable seafarers, the appearance of a dolphin frolicking in a bow wave may well have seemed like a messenger from the gods or an omen from Poseidon. In a way, the oceans created their own mythology and the creatures that populated the wild waters became entwined with the lives of men.

The scientific term for whales and dolphins—Cetacea—is derived from the mythical Greek sea monsters known as the Ketea. Oppian Halieutica, a third-century Geek poet, described them thus:

"The Ketea are mighty of limb and huge, the wonders of the sea, heavy with strength invincible, a terror for the eyes to behold and ever armed with deadly rage—many of these there be that roam the spacious seas, where are the unmapped prospects of Poseidon, but few of them come night the shore, those only whose weight the beaches can bear and whom the salt water does not fail."

In terms of a whale with an actual character, Moby Dick is perhaps the most famous whale in the world, albeit a literary construct. Herman Melville's novel, first published in 1851 under the title *The Whale*, was inspired by two actual events, the first being the sinking of the Nantucket whaling ship *Essex* by a large sperm whale, which rammed it 3,700km (2,000 miles) off the western coast of South America. Owen Chase, first mate and one of eight survivors, wrote of his experiences in his 1821 *Narrative of the Most Extraordinary and Distressing Shipwreck of the Whale-Ship Essex*. Lemuel Shaw, Melville's son-in-law, managed to find a copy of the book, which by that time was out of print, and bought it for him. Then there was actually an albino sperm whale called Mocha Dick which was killed in 1830 off the Chilean island of Mocha. Maddened by dozens of harpoons protruding from his back and sides, testimony to the persistent attempts of whalers, Mocha Dick often attacked ships with premeditated ferocity. Swedish whalers also claimed to have killed a very old white whale in 1859, and a Nantucket whaler claimed to have harpooned a white whale in 1902. Whale boats were often attacked by whales, and at times the mother ships were also attacked. These tales were meat and drink to Melville in his literary quest to describe the life and times of the whalers and to weave a story of the great white whale and the crazed vendetta of the *Pequod*'s Captain Ahab, urging his crew on with promises of gold: "Whosoever of ye raises me that same white whale, he shall have this gold ounce, my boys!"

Without doubt whales and dolphins have played a central role in the mythology of humankind. However, this relationship ultimately became a one-sided affair, with the odds stacked in favour of the humans. The arrival of humans has always coincided with the decimation of the large fauna of the areas they settled— America, Australia and New Zealand being prime examples. Africa did not suffer these predations due to the co-evolution of man with the fauna of that continent. On a smaller scale, the sobering and tragic story of the Mauritian dodo has reached the dubious status of having made its way into the English language as an idiomatic expression—'as dead as a dodo'. The oceans, however, were less accessible for humankind and it took the development of a certain level of technology before man could venture out on the sea. It also took a special breed of men to hunt whales in open boats on the high seas, particularly in high latitudes where cold, darkness and ice were constant threats. In spite of the hardships, these old-time whalers managed to decimate whale populations to the extent that, between 1785 and 1805, British, American and French whaling ships killed an estimated 12,000 whales between Walvis Bay and Delagoa Bay (Maputo). The populations collapsed, particularly due to the main target being mothers and calves. Shore-based whaling carried on in spite of the low stock levels right through into the twentieth century. The last attempt to take a whale from an open boat with a hand harpoon was in False Bay in 1929, by which time an estimated 1,580 right whales had been taken from the shore by South Africans—which was a minor fraction of the total kills by all nations from this stock.

Twentieth-century technology assisted in improving the kill rate. The slaughter became more automated and extended to other species of whale, which had been off limits due to their tendency to sink. The new harpoons allowed air to be pumped into the animals and with this new 'advance' all the great whales of the world's oceans became fair game. In 1908, steel-hulled ships began hunting in South African waters. However, population levels were so low along the South African coastline that only a total of 84 whales were taken over a period of thirty years—an average of less than three per year. However, on the international front, particularly after World War II, factory ships, with attendant whale hunters, allowed for the decimation of the whale pods to the extent that perhaps only 300 northern right whales now exist in the North Atlantic and North Pacific. The plight of the blue whale is not much better—they are perhaps one of the rarest creatures on earth, and it is not known if they will be able to claw back the lost ground to ensure their long-term survival. For the blue whale to go extinct would be a tragedy, for at over 30m in length and magnificent in its enormity, this beautiful animal is the largest creature ever to inhabit the Earth.

Cetacean intelligence

Brain development is measured by the ratio of brain weight to body weight, a ratio called cephalization. Humans, whales and dolphins are on the same level on the cephalization coefficient scale. This is not the only criteria for the assessment of intelligence, however, and behavioural aspects of the animal also need to be taken into account. Elephants have large brains but cannot be included in the discussion on higher intelligent beings due to behavioural and communication characteristics.

Humans and Cetacea have the same basic brain components, namely the old, reptilian brain, the palaeomammalian brain, and the neocortex. The neocortex is the convoluted grey layer covering the cerebral hemispheres, which in humans takes up almost half of the brain. This, along with the degree of cortical lamination, has become accepted criteria for determining brain development and the complexity of thought processes. An excellent example of the development of the cerebral capacity of Cetacea is found in modern river dolphins. These creatures swim far inland along flooded river systems during the tropical rainy season in search of fish. However, they must retain in their memory a detailed map of the waterways, so as not to become stranded when the flood waters recede. They also need to communicate within their social group and have developed echolocation and tactile senses as a means of doing so, as muddy waters hinder visual communication between individuals. The brains of the river dolphins are approximately the size of Homo erectus, the first real human, who appeared about two million years ago. In contrast, the river dolphin developed his present-day brain size 30 million years ago. The seafaring Cetaceans, however, developed even larger brains, possibly due to the pressures of the marine environment. However, these pressures may not account entirely for the massive growth in brain capacity and it is considered that the challenges of communicating through the vast oceans may have spurred this growth. In short, social and sexual pressures led to increased brain growth in the seafaring Cetaceans, building on the evolutionary advances made by early riverine dolphins.

Compare this to the development of intelligence in humans, who evolved from an apelike ancestor. As in the Cetacea, the brain was not totally reorganized, but the newer parts of the brain (e.g. the palaeomammalian over the reptilian) layered over the older. When our early ancestors moved from the east African forests out onto the open savannah, their brain size was forced to increase rapidly in order to survive, possibly due to the need for communication and language development. Increased brain size then led to the development of technology, but the long and short of it is that our brain evolved much faster than that of the Cetacea. At a time when whales and dolphins had brains comparable to their present size, ours were the size of the tree shrew, our earliest primate ancestor.

There are many old whalers' and fishermen's tales concerning the intelligence of Cetacea encountered in the sea. One such tale was related to a Dr John Lilly of the Whaling Institute by a visiting scientist. During the whaling season in the Antarctic, a group of several thousand orcas were playing with a fleet of commercial fishing boats. They were killing the fish near the boats, and the fleet could catch no fish. The fishermen radioed the whaling fleet for assistance. The fleet sent over a few boats armed with harpoon guns, one of which fired at and killed an orca. Within half an hour, all the whales disappeared from within a 25-mile radius of the whaling boats, although the fishing boats that were not aided by the whaling boats were still being bothered by the orcas. What is of special interest in this story is that both the fishing and whaling boats were World War II corvettes, and the only distinctive difference was the harpoon gun mounted on the bows of the whaling boats. For the whales to differentiate between the two, and to tell their fellow orcas about it, entailed some mode of communication. This communication would be different from the kind displayed, for example, by a school of fish when encountering some dangerous phenomenon. Here, the lead fish would somehow say, "Turn right!" and all would turn right; the command being quick, the execution immediate. A different type of communication must have gone on between the whales when the dying whale or observer whales sent out the message such as: "There's a thing sticking out of a few boats which can kill us and haul us in. Avoid all boats with this projection!" The command is fairly complicated and it also requires the understanding of the hearers, their ability to differentiate between the two boats, and a memory because they avoided the whaling boats for many hours.

Dolphins' brains are second only to that of humans in terms of size. A bottlenose dolphin's brain is approximately one and a half times that of a man's and has a mass of 1.75kg. Studies of a dolphin's brain have shown that the area controlling hearing is very large, the area governing sight is somewhat smaller, and those areas controlling touch and smell are considerably reduced. The question is, how intelligent are they? It is extremely difficult to carry out intelligence tests on dolphins as they cannot speak or write, and have no hands to manipulate objects or levers. However, in oceanaria worldwide they are known for their ability to carry out complex tasks using echolocation and vision, all of which suggest high intelligence. Studies of dolphin 'language' have been carried out by a number of people over the years but they have still to come up with insights into this language, although several sounds have been associated with particular meanings. The jury is still out as to whether dolphins are capable of communicating on a level any more advanced than that of chimpanzees or elephants, although based on the orca account given earlier it would appear that they may well be able to do so.

The whaling industry

Humans' record in terms of whaling is, much like our record elsewhere, a significant blot on our copy book. Whales and dolphins are central to the ancient myths of many different nations—whether as part of tribal folklore or mainstream literary classics such as Herman Melville's *Moby Dick*. The killing of Cetaceans is a trust betrayed, and somehow the irony is lost upon us, where we revere these creatures on one hand and slaughter them mercilessly on the other. Technically advanced, civilized nations still campaign for the resumption of whaling, and some of them continue to hunt whales in spite of public opinion and no fundamental need for whale products in our modern world.

A statistic in a 1969 Life Nature Library book, *The Sea*, gives a figure of 36,390 whales slaughtered in Antarctic waters in one year alone. It is estimated that New England whalers killed 100,000 right whales during the nineteenth century. An even more staggering statistic concerns grey whale populations—estimated at 25,000 in 1840, by the late 1930s barely 100 remained. That figure does indeed read '100'. Equally shocking, a 150-man crew, wading through eight tons of blood, could butcher a 30m-long blue whale in an hour—producing 50 tons of meat, 22 tons of bones, 2,000 pounds of liver, and 23 tons of blubber—all of which could be sold at vast profit back in home ports. In fact, it was a multi-million-dollar business, with factory ships, spotter helicopters, tankers, and attendant catcher boats taking to the seas to hunt these magnificent creatures almost to the brink of extinction.

Whale populations worldwide had collapsed before the outbreak of war in 1939. In 1946, the International Convention for the Regulation of Whaling led to the formation of the International Whaling Commission

(IWC), which in turn led to some protection for whales. There are still no international regulations to protect whales except for those of the IWC, and these regulations are amended annually and apply to member countries only. There are caveats within the regulations that allow for non-compliance in some instances. The IWC has no authority over non-member countries and regulates only the killing of great whales and a few smaller species. For the remaining species of small whales and dolphins, there is no international control over killing.

By 1972, with ongoing slaughter still taking place, a United Nations Environmental Programme (UNEP) meeting took place where 53 countries voted to end commercial whaling, 12 nations abstained and none voted against the motion. Back at the IWC this proved impossible to implement due to political and financial interests until 1982, when 25 countries voted to phase out commercial whaling over a three-year period. Seven nations opposed it; five abstained. Japan, Norway, Peru and the then Soviet Union entered an objection to the majority vote. Peru withdrew its objection at the IWC 1983 meeting, Japan withdrew her objection in 1986 and the Soviet Union halted commercial whaling at the end of its 1987 season. Norway has still to withdraw its objections. Some whaling nations have threatened to leave the IWC in spite of the fact that they have recognized whales as international animals. Pressure from lobby groups in the US has led to sanctions being imposed on countries that refuse to cease commercial whaling.

Between 1972 and 1980, Japan supported non-IWC or 'pirate' whaling activities and purchased products from the various operators. Only due to NGO conservation organizations investigating pirate operations and lobbying their respective governments to shut down the operations did the 'host' countries move against pirate whalers operating from within their territory. Japan provided the market for illicit whale produce, with minke whale meat contributing between 2.6 and 3.8 percent of Japan's annual protein consumption.

Whale products have been used for centuries and have found their way into cosmetics, adhesives, hormones, vitamins, medicines, oils, fertilizers, ivory and meat for animal and human consumption. However, there are modern-day substitutes for all whale products and there is absolutely no need for the killing of whales. Since 2 December 1971, the US has banned all whale products and South Africa, being party to the Convention on International Trade in Endangered Species (CITES), no longer trades in whale products. Astonishingly, the European Union only banned whale products as late as 1 January 1982. In 1983, CITES members approved the suspension of trade in all produce from whales for which the IWC was setting zero-catch limits, thereby reinforcing the hand of the IWC. Japan and Norway continue to campaign to have this suspension lifted.

Durban ran one of the largest land-based whaling stations in the world until it was shut down in 1975. Thousands of whales were caught off the coast and towed back to the port to be processed into a range of products for the local and overseas market. The industry started in 1907 when the Norwegian consul, Jacob Egeland, and Johan Bryde formed the South African Whaling Company, with two ships, in order to hunt whales. They started hunting in 1908 and killed 106 whales that year. The whalers shot the animals with a 165-pound metal harpoon loaded with explosive, which would kill the whale. The whale would then be pumped full of air and left to float. Several more whales would be killed, and once the hunting was over, the whales would be towed right into the bay, back into the harbour, and pulled out of the water via a slipway. Once in the processing plant, they were flensed, which means that all the blubber and flesh was stripped from the bones. The blubber was rendered down to oil, which was used to make soap, margarine and cooking fat, while the flesh was sold for human and animal consumption, and the bones ground down for bone and protein meal as well as meat extract and soup flavourings. The stench from the whaling station was so bad that the residents began to complain, and after the first whaling season it was decided to move the station to the seaward side of the bluff where there were fewer residents to complain. Whales were then loaded onto a purpose-built train, the only one of its kind in the world, and hauled over to the whaling station for processing. The whale line was about 1.5 miles from the slipway to the whaling station and the whales were carried on two flatbed carriages, which were able to carry one large whale or two smaller ones. The train was operated by the South African Railways and Harbours, who ran all South Africa's rail network at the time, and they charged by weight of animals hauled to the processing plant. As such, some accurate measurements of whale weights were taken, which are useful from a scientific point of view and perhaps the only real, long-lasting benefit of what was a bloody business. Most of the whaling companies collapsed due to World War I, but some started up again in 1919. In 1937 a factory ship, the *Uniwaleco*, began to operate out of Durban, making forays to the Antarctic with a number of catchers to hunt during the summer season. During the winter months, it moved up to Madagascar to hunt humpback whales. She was requisitioned by the navy during the war and sunk by an enemy torpedo. A second factory ship called the *Empire Victory* was purchased and Antarctic trips resumed. The trips were highly successful, catching up to 2,200 whales in a trip. However, populations were starting to collapse due to unrestricted whaling by all of the world's whaling nations, and the ship was sold to the Japanese. The land-based whaling didn't cease, however, and new technology was brought in—this time an aeroplane to spot the whales from the air, which was apparently highly successful. It was recorded that the aeroplane spotted 11,874 whales and that nearly half of these were killed by the catchers.

Whaling ceased in South Africa in 1976, mainly due to a collapse in whale populations and the soaring cost of fuel, rather than due to any change of heart, but South Africa continued to oppose a moratorium on commercial whaling. An apparent slight change of conscience in 1981 led her to abstain at the next IWC meeting, and did so again in 1982 when it came to vote on the three-year phase-out of commercial whaling. Behind the scenes the Dolphin Action and Protection Group had launched a national 'Save the Whales' campaign in 1979 and for 22 years sought to change the official South African view that whales were an exploitable marine resource than could be harvested rationally. The DAPG, in one of its many landmark achievements, managed to get the official view changed in 2001, the South African government announcing that it had changed its policy on commercial whaling and no longer supported lethal exploitation of whales. In fact, the decision makers went one step further, lending support to the formation of whale sanctuaries and the non-lethal use of whales for tourism, education and science. During research for this book, it was astonishing to find that these reversals of policy came so late in the day, particularly in view of the acknowledged slaughter that had taken place and the depleted stocks of whales in the world's oceans.

Whale evolution

In 1883, a short 24 years after Charles Darwin published his *Origin of the Species*, which in those Victorian times offended the religious sensibilities of much of Britain and elsewhere, fellow scientist William Flower focused this powerful new theory on one of the toughest problems in zoology—the whale. It had long been realized that whales were mammals and that they exhibited a host of characteristics that linked them to land-dwelling animals. How evolution had managed to craft such a unique beast presented a mystery as vast as the creature itself. His theory was that whales had evolved from a group of mammals known as ungulates, creatures whose best-known characteristic is hoofed feet. Dolphins, porpoises, orcas and all the great whales were closely related to cows, horses and pigs! Preposterous notions indeed. However, since then, palaeontologists, biologists and zoologists, after several decades of scientific endeavour, are convinced that Flower was right, and that whales and dolphins are indeed the progeny of hoofed animals.

It is accepted that the oceans were the cradle of life in the Proterozoic 3.85 billion years ago, and from simple, single-celled organisms called archaea or archaeabacteria, all subsequent life evolved. When life ventured out of the oceans it was betting on some long odds, and as Bill Bryson succinctly puts it: "We happen to belong to the portion of living things that took the rash but venturesome decision 400 million years ago to crawl out of the seas and become land-based and oxygen-breathing. In consequence, no less than 99.5 per cent of the world's habitable space by volume, according to one estimate, is fundamentally—in practical terms completely—off limits to us." Cetaceans have retaken the lost ground so to speak by returning to the oceans with all its attendant benefits.

Proto-whales were terrestrial creatures with fur and hooves. Their successors in the Eocene probably evolved into a stout, heavy-headed species, which pursued an amphibious life in the shallows. The early Eocene epoch, which lasted from 55 million years ago to around 34 million years ago, is often called the dawn of the age of mammals, and the time when whales had their first known beginnings. Allow for the passage of ten million years and these creatures were adapted to life in the oceans. This is fine in theory, but the question remains as to which animals were the ancestors of Cetaceans. Long-extinct ungulates called mesonychids were considered to be ancestors of modern whales, based on discoveries of whale fossils. However, DNA studies seem to indicate that whales arose from artiodactyls, a group that includes hippos, and that hippos are the closest living relatives to whales. Clearly then, there is some disagreement as to whale ancestry, although morphological similarities of ankle bones seem to support the hippo link.

Hans Thewissen, an anatomist and palaeontologist at the Northern Ohio Universities Colleges of Medicine, discovered the bones of a creature, which he called Pakicetus, in the Kuldana formation of northern Pakistan. Pakistan and India have seen the discovery of a number of fossils that are significant to the study of whales. During the Eocene, an ancient seaway called the Tethys Sea was located between the southern Gondwana supercontinent and its Eurasian counterpart. This seaway ultimately closed when India and Africa collided with the northern continent, thrusting up the towering peaks of the Alps, Hindu Kush and Himalayas, leaving only the Mediterranean Sea as the remnant of a larger ocean. It was in the Tethys Sea that whales evolved, and it is for this reason that many of the early whale fossils are preserved in Pakistan and India, thrust up from their resting place by the juddering forces of continents in collision.

Pakicetus shows very primitive skull and skeleton characteristics and is currently the earliest, best-preserved early Cetacean discovered to date. The creature had relatively well-developed limbs but was aquatic. The term 'whale' here is loosely applied as it certainly did not have the typical morphology normally associated with the whales. It does, however, satisfy the requirements for being a whale Cetacean due to the arrangement of cusps on its molars, the folding of a bone in the middle ear, and the positioning of ear bones within the skull. All these features are peculiar to whales of the late Eocene but absent in land mammals. Studies have shown that the specialized inner ear of whales developed early in their evolution, which assisted them in becoming fully aquatic. The development comprises a semicircular canal within the inner ear, which maintains the balance of the animal and evolved approximately 45 million years ago. It allows Cetaceans to perform highly acrobatic swimming manoeuvres without becoming disorientated or dizzy, and was one of a number of several defining events that removed the need to return to the land.

A million years after Pakicetus, a new arrival took up residence on the ocean margins. In 1994, Thewissen discovered fossil remains of *Ambulocetus natans*—'the walking swimming whale'—in Pakistan. It had a squat and powerful build, sharp teeth and was approximately the size of a large sea lion. The teeth and ears were similar to more modern whales, indicating that this creature was semi-aquatic. Further digs in India's Rann of Kutch produced a host of additional fossils known as the protocetids which added to our understanding of whale evolution. Forty-two million years ago, the area was a green, shifting delta, which was periodically drowned by influxes of the Tethys Sea. Fossil shark, ray, bony fish, turtle and crocodile fossil skeletons occur in abundance, along with the skeletons of early whales who were experimenting with life in the oceans. Whale ancestors found here have been given inaccessible names like Indocetus, Rodhocetus, Andrewsiphius and Kutchicetus.

During this time, there were various advances and developments in whale morphology and anatomy, which assisted in their transition from land to sea. One of the great advances in whale evolution was the migration of nostrils from the tip of their snouts towards the top of their heads. Modern whales can surface, exhale, inhale and dive again without stopping or having to tilt their snout to breathe. Pakicetus' nostrils were located at the business end of its snout, while Rodhocetus' nostrils were higher on its skull, halfway between those of its ancestors and modern whales. In addition to the migration of nostrils, other adaptations to life in the oceans took place. The spinal column became stronger and increasingly flexible, while the rear limbs and hip bones atrophied. Their necks became shorter, which assisted in reducing drag, while their forelegs became flipper-like rudders. Outer ears had all attendant difficulties of any other mammal taking to the sea, and as a result these fell into disuse, but with a parallel development of sensitive lower jaw bones which were able to pick up sounds underwater and transmit these to the inner ear via specialized fat pads. Each new species became increasingly more refined and able to spend more time at sea. This transition took less than ten million years and according to Thewissen, "Whales underwent the most dramatic and complete transformation of any mammal."

Protocetids were the first whales to leave the Indian subcontinent and disperse to all shallow (sub)tropical oceans of the world. In addition to Indo-Pakistan, they were also active around Africa and the east coast of North America. Protocetids ranged in length from 1.5m (5ft) to 5m (15ft) and looked like large-headed sea lions or walruses with webbed feet and protruding teeth. They were still, however, partially tied to the terrestrial world, returning to mate and give birth. However, these ties were to become increasingly tenuous, and oxygen-isotope analyses of their teeth indicate that they no longer required fresh drinking water. Without this requirement, the descendants of *Ambulocetus* had crossed a crucial metabolic threshold, clearing the way to them becoming fully seagoing marine mammals, unshackled by any need to return to the land.

Approximately 40 million years ago, as the ancient whales spread out from the Tethys Sea, a group known as the durodontines arose. These creatures could still bend their flippers at the elbow and their nostrils had only migrated halfway up their snout, but in almost all other respects were ocean-going Cetaceans that gave birth at sea. The final link to the land had been broken. Durodontines may have been the dynasty that went on to produce modern whales. Durodontines and their close relatives the Basilosaurids were enormous, reaching lengths up to 20m (60ft), with long, serpentine-like bodies. They had tail flukes but probably swam using sinuous body movements. Durodontines on the other hand propelled themselves using their flukes. In spite of the evolution of tail flukes, both basilosaurids and durodontines had complete sets of hind limbs, including knees and toes. Both species, however, lacked the 'melon' organ which allowed their descendants to sing and use echolocation. This was to be the next development in whale anatomy, adding another device in their ongoing evolutionary development, leading ultimately to eventual dominance over the world's oceans.

EVOLUTION

The density of seawater is 800 times that of air, which allows it to transmit sound far more efficiently than air. In addition, sound will travel 5.5 times further in a watery medium, properties which Cetaceans use extensively in their communications, navigation and location of food. Whale vocalizations comprise a variety of clicks, whistles and calls and the sounds are emitted through the whale's melon-shaped forehead, and are reflected back off objects, and received via their lower jaws, which have an open, cell-like construction. These reflections build up an auditory 'image' similar to a bat's echolocation system. James Goedert has been fossil hunting in the American northwest for the last 20 years, focusing his attention on the Oligocene, which extends from 34 to 24 million years ago. Some of the first evidence of echolocation has been found in these rocks, the evidence comprising the beginnings of special air sacs that led off the main nasal passage, used for moving air back and forth to create sound vibrations, and a melon—the lens of fatty tissue in the whale's forehead being used for focusing transmitted sounds. Finally, thinned portions of the lower jaw aided in reception of sound signals. These were fundamental advances, echolocation giving whales the ability to navigate and find prey and increase their success as a species, particularly for toothed whales. Baleen whales on the other hand are known to use low frequencies to communicate, sometimes over long distances. Some of the first evidence of echolocation was found in squalodons, which lived from 33 to 14 million years ago. They belong to the family of toothed whales and comprise a strange mix of archaic and modern features. They had very complex dentition, which harks back to more primitive forms, but also exhibit compressed craniums and some of the first appearances of echolocation, which are characteristics of more modern forms. For many decades, it was thought that the squalodontids represented original stock from which most of our modern odontocetes (toothed whales) evolved thanks to the presence of both primitive and modern characteristics, but this view has changed, and it is likely that squalodontids have little to do with the ancestry of modern dolphins.

The development of echolocation is considered to have been the driving force in the increase in size of Cetacean brains. The amount of brain mass related to the total body mass of an animal is defined as encephalization, with the argument being that the greater the degree of encephalization, the greater the level of intelligence of the animal. This theory was propounded as early as 1871, by no less than Charles Darwin himself, who wrote in *The Descent of Man*: "No one, I presume, doubts that the large proportion which the size of man's brain bears to his body, compared to the same proportion in the gorilla or orang, is closely connected with his mental powers."

One of the major hypotheses concerning the high degree of encephalization in toothed whales, including dolphins, is based on the need of the animal to process high volumes of neural data. This data is generated by the echolocation equipment of the animals, whereby auditory pulses are generated, reflected and received, and then processed to create the auditory 'picture', which allows for navigation and feeding. Clearly, fast and accurate processing of this information is highly advantageous for the animal, and these pressures or stimuli led to a rapid increase in brain size.

At some stage in the evolution of whales came a split that divided them into the mysticetes—baleen whales—and the odontocetes, which are the original toothed whales. The mysticetes use baleen plates— comb-like plates, which descend from the roof of the whale's mouth—to strain food from seawater. Baleen whales have toothed ancestors, and whereas toothed whales have full sets of teeth, baleen whales have teeth in the early foetal stage, but lose them before they are born. However, the presence of teeth in the foetal stage is good evidence for a common toothed-whale ancestor. In fact, a late Oligocene whale, Aetiocetus, one of the earliest examples of baleen whales, also possessed a full set of teeth.

Mysticetes were quite diverse during the Oligocene, 30 to 23 million years ago. Toothed mysticetes have been found from scattered localities, but by 30 million years ago the first toothless baleen whales—the cetotheres—had evolved. They had baleen in a thin, flat, upper jaw, and a cylindrical toothless, lower jaw that is very similar to modern examples, but otherwise were quite primitive. Primitive features included a blow hole nearer the snout, a less advanced ear region and less compression of the neck vertebrae. These early cetotheres more than likely included the ancestors of modern rorquals. James Goedert's work has produced the oldest odontocetes, a number of early mysticetes, and the North Pacific's oldest whale—studies which have assisted in bridging the knowledge gap between the Eocene and the Miocene. The remains of Aetiocetus help to bridge the gap between ancient and baleen whales, with teeth as well as signs of skin tissue on its widened upper jaw, which is an indication of baleen plate development. Palaeontologist Lawrence Barnes of the Natural History Museum of Los Angeles County has discovered 30 species of Cetaceans, including eight species of cetotheres. The discoveries were made at Sharktooth Hill, near Bakersfield, California, in an area rich in Miocene fossils, dating from 24 to five million years ago. The cetotheres survived right through to three million years ago, co-existing with modern bowheads and northern right whales. With time, the cetotheres were succeeded by the rorquals that were more streamlined and faster.

Faunal changes that led to the evolution of modern mysticetes from early ancestors have been correlated with environmental and physical changes in the oceans. Some of these changes included the establishment of a West Antarctic ice sheet, partial closure of the western opening of the Mediterranean Sea and closure of the Indo-Pacific Seaway, all of which may have contributed to falling temperatures, steep temperature gradients and increased complexity in ocean currents. These environmental changes led to changes in the variety of pelagic habitats and the partitioning of food resources. In the same way that earlier ocean current changes resulted in the radiation of archaic mysticetes (cetotheres) during the early and middle Oligocene, another major shift in ocean currents and sea temperatures may have brought about the demise of the archaic forms.

A number of questions still exist concerning the evolution of whales and the whale family tree is far from being finished. However, we have a far better understanding of whale evolution than we had even ten years ago. DNA analyses show that there are proteins and amino acids common to both whales and artiodactyls— the pigs and hippos of our modern world. This is borne out by similarities in ankle bones between the species, discovered by Dr Philip Gingerich and colleagues and described in a 2001 copy of *Science*. These creatures, the anthracotheres, common in Eurasia during the early age of mammals, led to the rise of a number of marsh-dwelling forms and ultimately the evolution of whales in all their majesty. As D. H. Chadwick of the *National Geographic* put it, "From the Miocene onwards, whales had evolved to the extent that they could take advantage of prey ranging from small fish to crustaceans, sea lions to giant squid. Their hunting range was from the shallow seas to the abyssal depths. They had severed the umbilical ties to the land—no longer did they need to drink fresh water or come ashore to mate or give birth. They were in short masters of the deep, having walked, waded, paddled and fluked their way to dominion over most of the blue planet."

South African ceteology

The Centre for Dolphin Studies

The Centre for Dolphin Studies (CDS) is an internationally recognized marine-mammal research institute, which was established in 1989 by its present director Dr Vic Cockcroft. The aim of the CDS is to promote and carry out research and conservation of marine mammals in southern African waters. The CDS was launched due to a lack of knowledge of western Indian Ocean Cetaceans and, more specifically, South African species. Added impetus was supplied by ongoing coastal degradation. The centre runs its own research and educational programmes as well as assisting in projects north of the border and other places in the world. These programmes are diverse and range from behavioural studies, ecology, taxonomy, conservation and marine management. To date, the CDS has completed in excess of 30 research programmes and published more than 145 scientific papers and popular articles.

The CDS also encourages the science of marine mammalogy through educational outreach programmes to school and university students. They also assist in providing the relevant authorities in neighbouring states with information necessary to effectively conserve and manage their marine mammals and coastal environments.

The CDS allies itself with the goals and aims of the World Conservation Union (IUCN) Species Survival Commission and in particular the Cetacean and Sirenian Specialist Groups. The close association of the CDS with a number of other institutions affords an inter/multidisciplinary approach, which results in an active and innovative programme of research on marine mammals and their habitat. The CDS's work has attained international recognition, which has opened the door to affiliations with both local and international universities (including: Nelson Mandela Metropolitan University, University of KwaZulu-Natal, University of Pretoria, Texas A&M University, University Eduardo Mondlane [Mozambique], Swire Institute, University of Hong Kong, University of St Andrews [Scotland], University of Central Florida, University of Tulear [Madagascar], Universidade Agostino Neto [Angola]) as well as numerous non-governmental organizations.)

The hard work of the CDS and its cultivation of relationships with other academic institutes has paid off, in that the centre has become the most productive dolphin research institute in the country, if not Africa. It has represented Africa at more than 49 local and international conferences and workshops. In recognition of the CDS's contribution to Cetacean studies and conservation, its director, Dr Vic Cockcroft, has been appointed one of a total of 30 experts in the world (one of only two African representatives) on the World Conservation Union's (IUCN) Cetacean and Sirenian Specialist Groups.

The CDS operates as an independent, non-profit research trust based out of Plettenberg Bay, where it carries out a range of research studies, promotes marine mammal awareness and is actively involved in conservation-orientated eco-tourism.

The Mammal Research Institute

The Mammal Research Institute is a subsidiary of the University of Pretoria. Its aim is to be internationally recognized for its research and teaching on the subjects of biology and ecology of African mammals. It also aims to focus on what is relevant to Africa, and to southern Africa in particular, with regard to conserving the diversity of the continent's indigenous mammal fauna in the context of sustainable human development. Professor Peter Best is attached to the institute but is far from being land-locked, being based at the South African Museum in Cape Town. He is a recognized international expert on Cetaceans, having published numerous journal articles on Cetaceans of the southern African and Southern oceans. He is still very much involved in field work and research after 40 years of Cetacean study, and has just published his latest book titled *Whales and Dolphins of the Southern African Subregion*, which is a veritable mine of information on all things Cetacean.

The Dolphin Action and Protection Group

Nan Rice was the founder of the Dolphin Action and Protection Group. In 1970, she was instrumental in bringing about legislation to protect dolphins from killing, capture and harassment in what was then the Cape Province. Under the 1973 Sea Fisheries Act, this protection was extended to SWA (now Namibia) and under the 1998 Marine Living Resources Act (Act No. 18 of 1998) was amended, based to some extent on the recommendations made by the Group. In 1978, she began to assist with investigations into 'pirate' whaling (whaling beyond the regulations of the International Whaling Commission). She provided valuable information for investigators, which was critical to bringing these shameful operations to an end. This information was subsequently incorporated into reports submitted to the International Whaling Commission (IWC) and the United States Senate Enquiry.

In 1979, the Group launched the 'Save the Whales' campaign in South Africa and, under the umbrella of this campaign, approached the government in the same year with substantive evidence that whales should receive protection in South African waters from killing, disturbance and harassment. On 5 December 1980, regulations were promulgated, but the whales were only protected in their breeding season. Once again the Group approached the authorities, and in 1984 the regulations were extended to protect the whales all year round.

After launching the 'Save the Whales' campaign, it took the Group over 20 years of uphill lobbying to change the government's vote at International Whaling Committee (IWC) meetings from pro- to anti-whaling. Not only the government, but at that time most South African citizens were not against commercial whaling, but through intensive educational programmes over the years attitudes towards these creatures have changed.

South Africa's regulations to protect Cetaceans are amongst the strictest in the world. The Group co-operates with the authorities to ensure that the regulations are properly implemented.

In 1979, the Group also launched the Dolphin Whale Watch RSA project. Data collected from observers enabled officers of the Group to write up several papers on the movements and behaviour of Cetaceans frequenting South African waters, two of which were published in a reputable scientific journal. The project was closed in 2005. During the time it was in operation, a mass of data was collected, which has helped the Group considerably in its work.

In 1984, the Group launched the 'Save Antarctica' campaign and joined the international Antarctic & Southern Ocean Coalition. For many years, serious campaign work was done to educate the public about Antarctica and the man-made threats to this continent, as well as investigations into Patagonian toothfish

SA CETEOLOGY

poaching. As officers of the Group served on the Sea Patrol Co-Ordinating Committee (SEAPACC) during the 1990s and into 2000, they were able to bring poaching problems to the attention of the SA Navy and other maritime organizations.

In 1988, the 'Save Our Sea Life: Prevent Plastic Pollution' campaign was launched in South Africa. Since that time, this campaign has involved thousands of South Africans and it was the first time an organization had tackled the problem seriously in South Africa. This has been one of the most successful campaigns run by the Group.

Under the umbrella of the foregoing campaign, fell the international issue of high seas pelagic drift-netting. The Group worked on this issue for several years, concentrating its efforts on the southern Indian and Atlantic oceans.

Among other things, the Group persuaded the South African government to promulgate anti-drift-netting regulations in 1989 and persuaded the government of Mauritius to do likewise in 1991. The United Nations brought about a moratorium on high seas pelagic drift-netting in 1992, thanks to the input and campaigning of hundreds of scientists and non-governmental organizations internationally, including the Group.

In 1991, through the Group's efforts and with the help of certain scientists, the government agreed to promulgate protection of the great white shark. This was a world first. Namibia followed South Africa's example in 1993, and subsequently numbers of other countries have done likewise. Protection of this apex predator has certainly changed attitudes towards sharks, despite unfortunate attacks.

For many years, the Group has trained a team of volunteers to assist at mass strandings of Cetaceans in the Western Cape. Information is also given to the public about both single and mass strandings, a subject that never fails to elicit interest.

In 2005, working with officers of Marine & Coastal Management (MCM), the Group helped form the South African Whale Disentanglement Network. In 2006, a two-day training workshop was organized, and to date this project has proven highly successful. No one, unless trained and recognized by MCM, is allowed to disentangle a whale. The Group has helped MCM to obtain the necessary equipment used during the disentanglement process and assists with administration work.

The DAPG also distributes educational literature, holds lectures, shows slides and films, takes part in radio and TV programmes, produces original articles, and supplies the media, organizations and individuals with contacts and information on Cetaceans. They also liaise with local and overseas conservation organizations and scientists.

The Whale Studio and International Fund for Animal Welfare

Hermanus boasts a series of beautiful information boards along the International Fund for Animal Welfare (IFAW) whale walk. These were designed and illustrated by Noel and Belinda Ashton of Oceans of Africa. Noel has been visiting Walker Bay for the last 30 years and has carried out extensive research on the various whale and dolphin species of South Africa's coastline. Based on this knowledge, he is able to paint the most exquisite and scientifically accurate paintings of whales and dolphins in their natural element. He is also an accomplished sculptor and produces sculptures of—you've guessed it—whales. The paintings of the IFAW whale walk were specially commissioned to best represent the different species that frequent these shores. Belinda supplies the text and layout, which assist in making the boards so visually appealing and, of course, educational.

The IFAW was founded in Canada in 1969 and is represented in 15 countries, with a subscription base of almost three million globally. It has for over 20 years been involved in whale protection and is currently one of the world's leading advocacy organizations for Cetaceans and the ocean environment. They are involved in scientific research on whale physiology, ecology and behaviour, and campaign at the IWC and other international forums.

West and southern coast accommodation and contacts	
A <R200, **B** R200 to R400, **C** R400 to R700, **D** >R700.	

Arniston

Clydesdale House (B)	Self Catering 028-424 1290 clydesdalehouse@telkomsa.net

Betty's Bay

Bucaco Sud Guest House (B)	Guest House 028-272 9628 bucaco@hermanus.co.za
La Cachette (B)	Guest House 028-272 9117 info@lacachette.co.za
The Retreat (B)	Guest House 028-272 9157 retreatbb@ananzi.co.za
Silverdunes (A)	Hotel 028-272 9100 info@silverdunes-accommodation. co.za

Bredasdorp

Overberg Tourism Bureau	028-214 1466 www.tourismcapeoverberg.com
General contacts	www.viewoverberg.com www.overberginfo.com www.overberg.co.za

Caledon

Overberg Tourism Bureau	028-214 1466 www.tourismcapeoverberg.com
General contacts	www.viewoverberg.com www.overberginfo.com www.overberg.co.za

Cape Agulhas

Cape Agulhas Tourism Bureau	**028-**424 2584 wwwtourismcapeagulas.co.za

Cape Hangklip

Hangklip-Kleinmond Tourism Bureau	028-271 5657 info@ecoscape.org.za www.ecoscape.org.za

Cape Town

Cape Town Tourism	021-487 6800 capetown@tourismcapetown.co.za www.tourismcapetown.co.za

Cape Town Tourism Centre	021-405 4500 welcome@tourcapetown.com
General contacts	www.capestay.co.za
De Hoop	
Buchu Bush Camp (B)	Guest House 028-542 1602 info@buchu-bushcamp.com
Doringbaai	
Thornbay Accommodation (A)	Self Catering 027-215 133 thornbay@telkomsa.net
Gansbaai	
Gansbaai Tourism	028-384 1439
Stille Runaway (B)	Self Catering 083-462 0820 jaco@stillerunaway.co.za
Sea Kaya (A)	Self Catering 083-294 2191 seakaya.seakaya@gmail.com
Cliff Lodge (C)	Guest House 028-384 0983 stay@clifflodge.co.za
Crayfish Lodge (C)	Guest House 028-384 1898 info@crayfishlodge.com
Kleinzee Ocean Front Guest House (B)	Guest House 083-650 5156 loumy@mweb.co.za
Elands Bay	
Straw Revolution (D for entire house)	Self Catering 027-789 0278 mark@strawrevolution.co.za
George	
George Tourism Office	044-801 9295 info@georgetourism.co.za www.georgetourism.co.za
Gordon's Bay	
General contacts	www.gordonsbay.com
Gordon's Bay Tourist & Accommodation Centre	021-856 5204 gordonsbayinfo@mweb.co.za www.gordonsbaytourism.com

Blue Marine (C)	Self Catering 021-856 5987 info@bluemarine.co.za
Manor on the Bay (B)	Self Catering 021-856 0845 highcliffe@mweb.co.za
La Dolce Vita (C)	Self Catering 021-913 1588 ladolcevita@keretaccommodation. co.za
Berg en Zee (B)	Guest House 021-856 3095 info@bergenzee.co.za
Gordons Beach Lodge (B)	Guest House 021-856 3519 info@gordonsbeachlodge.co.za
Groot Brakrivier	
Great Brak River Museum and Information Centre	044-620 3338 gbrtourism@gmail.com www.greatbrakriver.co.za
Skalpa (C)	Self Catering 044-879 2065 skalpa@mweb.co.za
Zesty (B)	Self Catering 082-495 2097 yvonne.jacobs@parexel.com
Hartenbos	
Mossel Bay Tourism Bureau	044-691 2202
Heidelberg	
Heidelberg Information Centre	028-722 2700 info@heidelberginfo.co.za www.heidelberginfo.co.za
Heidelberg Tourism Bureau	028-722 1917 hbmun@malan.co.za
Broodkas Ranch (B)	Guest House 028-713 2882 broodkas@telkomsa.net
Hermanus	
Hermanus Tourism	028-312 2629 www.hermanus.co.za
Hermanus Backpackers (A)	Backpackers 028-312 2629

La Fontaine (C)	Bed & Breakfast 028-313 4595 lafont@hermanus.co.za
Auberge Baleens (A)	Bed & Breakfast 028-313 1201 baleens@capequest.co.za
Nautilus Cottage (D)	Bed & Breakfast 028-313 4955 nautiluscottage@hermanus.co.za
Whale Cottage (C)	Bed & Breakfast 028-313 0929 hermanus@whalecottage.com
Kennedy's Beach Villa (D)	Hotel 028-316 2169 kennedys@hermanus.co.za
The Marine (D)	Hotel 028-313 1000 hermanus@relaischateaux.com
Hout Bay	
General contacts	www.houtbayonline.com
Kalk Bay	
General contacts	www.gokalkbay.co.za
Klein Brakrivier	
General contacts	www.littlebrakriver.co.za
Kleinmond	
Hangklip-Kleinmond Tourism Bureau	028-271 5657 info@ecoscape.org.za www.ecoscape.org.za
General contacts	www.kleinmond.com www.kleinmondprop.co.za
Villa Sikelela (C)	Self Catering 021-434 9245 info@sikelela.com
Seefeld (B)	Self Catering 082-654 5529 jag@globalrem.co.za
The Homestead (A)	Self Catering 083-759 4220 reservations@the-homestead.co.za
Knysna	
Knysna Tourism Bureau	044-382 5510 knysna.tourism@pixie.co.za www.visitknysna.com

Lake Pleasant (C)	Self Catering 044-349 2400 reservations@lakepleasantliving.com
Phantom River View (B)	Self Catering 021-702 2302 info@phantomforest.com
Woodcutters Forest Lodges (B)	Self Catering 044-389 0044 archan@cyberpark.co.za
The Lofts Boutique Hotel (C)	Hotel 044-302 5710 thelofts@theboatshed.co.za
Kommetjie	
General contacts	www.kommetjie.co.za
Lambert's Bay	
Lambert's Bay Tourism Office	027-432 1000 lambertsinfo@mweb.co.za www.lambertsbay.co.za
Langebaan	
Langebaan Tourism Association	022-772 1515 www.langebaaninfo.co.za
Langebaan House Boats (B)	Self Catering 021-689 9718 langebaanhouseboats@mweb.co.za
Samos (B)	Self Catering 083-235 3316 weekendholidays@telkomsa.net
Helios Place (A)	Self Catering 021-8723100 heliosplace@telkomsa.net
Llandudno	
General contacts	www.llandudno.co.za
Malgas	
Mudlark Riverfront Lodge (B)	Guest House 028-542 1161 info@mudlark.co.za
Tides River Lodge (B)	Guest House 028-542 1018 tideslodge@dsm.co.za
Melkbosstrand	
General contacts	www.melkbos.com

At Atlantic Splendour (D)	Self Catering 021-482 1160 jj@div.co.za
Villa Cintra (D)	Self Catering 084-553 0003 joannel@escapetownvillas.com
Apartment 2 Rent (A)	Self Catering 021-856 4777 una@mweb.co.za
Bontop B&B (B)	Bed & Breakfast 021-553 4192 info@bontkop.co.za
Sandcastle B&B (B)	Bed & Breakfast 021-553 1607 info@thesandcastle.co.za
Two Owls Guest House (A)	Bed & Breakfast 021-553 3925 twoowls@telkomsa.net
Mossel Bay	
African Oceans Manor On The Beach (B)	Self Catering 044-695 1846 info@africanoceans.co.za
Siesta Sea Cottage (C)	Self Catering 021-424 7752 johannes_c@worldonline.co.za
Muizenberg	
General accommodation	www.muizenberg.info
Blue Bottle Guest House (B)	Self Catering/Bed & Breakfast 022-788 1600 bluebottle@wol.co.za
Villa D'Algarve (B)	Guest House 022-424 8981 info@arnolds.co.za
Napier	
Napier Tourism Bureau	028-423 3325 napierinfo@telkomsa.net
Peace Valley Guest House (B)	Guest House 028-423 3372 info@peacevalleyguesthouse.co.za
Noordhoek	
Noordhoek Tourism	021-789 2812 www.noordhoektourism.co.za

Blue Tangerine (C)	Guest House 021-785 3156 info@bluetangerine.co.za
Sacred Mountain Lodge (B)	Guest House 021-789 2713 info@sacredmountain.co.za
Bazara (B)	Guest House 083-389 7951 bazara@holidaylets.co.za
African Violet (C)	Self Catering 021-785 2836 reservations@africanviolet.co.za
Pine Ridge Farm (C)	Self Catering 021-789 2377 info@pineridgefarm.co.za
Clydesdale (A)	Self Catering 021-789 2796 clydesdale@webafrica.org.za
Afton Grove (C)	Guest House 021-785 2992 info@afton.co.za
Ou skip	
Ou skip Holiday Resort	Resort 021-553 2058 ouskip@intekom.co.za www.ouskip.co.za
Paternoster	
Blue Dolphin (B)	Guest House 022-752 2001 info@bluedolphin.co.za
Paternoster Dunes (B)	Guest House 022-752 2214 reservations@paternosterdunes.co.za
Tussen Duine (C)	Guest House 021-797 4943 tussenduine@mweb.co.za
Plettenberg Bay	
Plettenberg Bay Tourism	044-533 4065 info@plettenbergbay.co.za www.plettenbergbay.co.za
Anlin Beach House (C)	Self Catering 044-533 3694 stay@anlinbeachhouse.co.za

Besalu Villa (C)	Self Catering 082-600 4600 nikkis@yebo.co.za
Bayside Lodge (B)	Self Catering 044-533 0601 stay@baysidelodge.co.za
The Plettenberg (D)	Hotel 044-533 2030 plettenberg@relaischateaux.com
Pringle Bay	
Overberg Tourism Bureau	028-214 1466 www.tourismcapeoverberg.com
General contacs	www.viewoverberg.com www.overberginfo.com www.overberg.co.za
Ashar Manor (B)	Self Catering 082-650 0291 wingedflowers@honpartner.co.za
Dune House (B)	Self Catering 083-250 8787 cindy@kingsley.co.za
Gecko House (B)	Self Catering 021-686 6491 info@capevacation.co.za
Moonstruck on Pringle Bay (C)	Guest House 028-273 8162 moonstruck@worldonline.co.za
Villa Marine (B)	Guest House 028-273 8081 villamarine@absamail.co.za
Hannah's View Guest House (B)	Guest House 028-273 8235 hannahsview@telkomsa.net
Riversdale	
Riversdale Tourism Bureau	028-713 1996 tourismrdale@isat.co.za www.riversdaleinfo.com
Riversonderend	
Overberg Tourism Bueau	028-214 1466 www.tourismcapeoverberg.com
General contacts	www.viewoverberg.com www.overberginfo.com www.overberg.co.za

Rooi Els	
Overberg Tourism Bureau	028-214 1466 www.tourismcapeoverberg.com
General contacs	www.viewoverberg.com www.overberginfo.com www.overberg.co.za
Sunset Bay (D)	Self Catering 028-271 5775 info@holidayscape.co.za
Sandown Bay	
Overberg Tourism Bureau	028-214 1466 www.tourismcapeoverberg.com
General contacts	www.viewoverberg.com www.overberginfo.com www.overberg.co.za
Shelley Point	
General contacts	www.pearlybeachonline.co.za www.danger-point-peninsula.co.za
Luxury Villa on the Beach (C)	Self Catering 022-742 1105 hof@bandenmarkt.com
Benign (B)	Self Catering 021-448 2998 info@benign.co.za
Corsica Villas (A)	Self Catering 022-742 1906 shelpoint@netactive.co.za
Oystercatcher Lodge (B)	Guest House 022-742 1202 ischristen@intekom.co.za
Simon's Town	
General contacts	www.simonstown.com www.gosimonstown.com
Boulders Beach Lodge (C)	Hotel 021-786 1758 boulders@iafrica.com
Central Hotel Guest House (B)	Hotel 021-786 3775 centralhotel@intekom.co.za
Lord Nelson Inn (C)	Hotel 021-786 3761 lordnelsonhotel@yahoo.com

Simon's Town Quayside Hotel (C)	Hotel 021-786 3838 quayside@relais.co.za
Topsail House (A)	Backpackers 021-786 5537 alondon@mweb.co.za
Simon's Town Backpackers (A)	Backpackers 021-786 7964 capipax@kingsley.co.za
Albatross House (B)	Bed & Breakfast 021-786 5906 albatrosshouse@absamail.co.za
Cali-Coco Terrace (B)	Bed & Breakfast 021-786 2300 calicoco@intekom.co.za
Cannon House (B)	Bed & Breakfast 021-786 4192 cannonhouse@tiscali.co.za
Whale View Manor (C)	Bed & Breakfast 021-786 3291 whaleview@tiscali.co.za
Somerset West	
General contacts	www.somersetwest.com
African Dreams (C)	Self Catering 021-855 5977 reinmuth@africandreams.za.net
Penny Lane (B)	Self Catering 021-852 9976 enquiries@pennylanelodge.co.za
Pinoaks (B)	Self Catering 021-851 2396 piekfam@worldonline.co.za
Ivory Heights (C)	Guest House 021-852 8333 info@ivoryheights.co.za
Dreamland (C)	Guest House 021-852 6259 dreamland@mweb.co.za
Blue Crane (B)	Guest House 021-852 4041 pagels@mweb.co.za
Straightway Head Boundary Hotel (C)	Hotel 021-851 7088 info@straightwayhead.com

St Helena Bay	
St Helena Bay Tourism Bureau	022-715 1142 bureau@kingsley.co.za
Elm Tree Guest Cottage (A)	Self Catering 022-736 1159 info@elmtreesa.com
Oystercatcher Lodge (B)	Guest House 022-742 1202 info@oystercatcher.co.za
Blueberry Holiday Flats (A)	Self Catering 022-742 1045 karoobiltong@telkomsa.net
Stanford	
General contacts	www.stanfordinfo.co.za
Elephant Hills (B)	Self Catering 021-689 7824 willsfamily@iafrica.com
Swellendam	
Swellendam Tourism Bureau	028-514 2770 infoswd@sdm.dorea.co.za www.swellendamtourism.co.za
Waterkloof Guest House (B)	Guest House 028-722 1811 info@waterkloofguesthouse.co.za
Old Mill Guest House (B)	Guest House 028-514 2790 guestcottage@oldmill.co.za
Bloomestate (C)	Guest House 028-514 2984 info@bloomestate.co
Klippe Rivier Country House (D)	Guest House 028-514 3341 res@klipperivier.com
Touwsrivier	
Touwsrivier Tourism Bureau	023-348 1192 info@routes.co.za www.routes.co.za/wc/touwsriver
Velddrif, Laaiplek and Dwarskersbos	
Velddrif Tourism Bureau	022-783 1821 velddriftoerisme@telkomsa.net
Laaiplek Hotel (B)	Hotel 022-783 1116 laaiplekhotl@telkomsa.net

Riviera Hotel (B)	Hotel 022-783 1137 rivierahotel@imaginet.co.za
Pelikaan Lodge (B)	Bed & Breakfast 022-783 2055 veldriftleon@vodamail.co.za
Sandveld (B)	Bed & Breakfast 022-783 0385 sandv@telkomsa.net
Dwaaihoek Lodge (B)	Bed & Breakfast 022-952 1170 info@draaihoek.com
Piet-my-Vrou (B)	Bed & Breakfast 022-783 1550
L'Amour (B)	Bed & Breakfast 022-783 0775 jophil@absamail.co.za
Riverside (B)	Bed & Breakfast 022-783 1865 www.riversidebb.co.za
Kom Dudu (B)	Bed & Breakfast 022-784 0121 komdudu@ebucksmail.com
Aflaaiplek (B)	Self Catering 082-809 6813 carl.joubert@mweb.co.za
Berg River Lodge (B)	Self Catering 022-783 0686
Wilderness	
Wilderness Tourism Bureau	044-877 0045 weta@wildernessinfo.co.za www.tourismwilderness.co.za
C Paradys Guest House (C)	Self Catering 044-877 0793 ceclia1@mweb.co.za
Heart Song (B)	Self Catering 044-877 0144 heartsong@mweb.co.za
Wilderness Views (B)	Self Catering 044-877 0783 puds@mweb.co.za
Witsand	
Witsand Tourism Bureau	028-537 1010 wact@telkomsa.net www.witsandtourism.co.za

Yzerfontein	
Yzerfontein Tourism	022-451 2366 www.tourismyzerfontein.co.za
La Villa (B)	Self Catering 022-451 2095 steint@mweb.co.za
Cong Balinese Beach House (C)	Self Catering sarah@isnet.co.za
Inglenook (C)	Self Catering 083-680 6800 inglenookchic@yahoo.co.za
Villa Pescatori (C)	Guest House 022-451 2782 angelique@villapescatori.co.za
Harbour View (B)	Guest House 022-451 2615 info@harbourviewbb.co.za
Lewens–Essens (B)	Guest House 022-451 2390 info@lewensessens.co.za

East cost accommodation and contacts	
A <R200, **B** R200 to R400, **C** R400 to R700, **D** >R700	
Durban	
General contacts	www.durban-venues.co.za www.durban.kzn.org.za www.durban-direct.com www.durban.co.za
Hibberdene	
Hibberdene Information Office	039-699 3203 hibberdene@hibuscuscoast.org.za
Ifafa Beach	
Ifafa Beach Holiday Resort	Resort 039-977 8615 www.ifafabeach.co.za
Port Shepstone & surrounds	
Mantis & Moon Backpackers (A)	Backpackers 039-684 6256 info@mantisandmoon.net
Banana Beach Holiday Resort (B)	Self Catering 039-681 3229 reservations@bananabeach.co.za
Oslo Beach Lodge (B)	Bed & Breakfast 039-685 4807 homeoff@venturenet.co.za
Dolphin Cove (B)	Bed & Breakfast 039-684 4807 erose@telkomsa.net
B Cubed Guesthouse (B)	Bed & Breakfast 039-684 3446 info@bcubedguesthouse.co.za
Kapenta Bay Hotel (C)	Hotel 039-682 5528 gm@kapentabay.co.za
Rocky Bay	
Rocky Bay Caravan Park	Caravan Park 039-976 0546 info@rockybay.co.za www.rockybay.co.za
Shelly Beach	
Emerald Cove (B)	Self Catering 039-315 5284 emerald@venturenet.co.za

Driftsands Holiday Flats (B)	Self Catering 039-315 0911 drift@venturenet.co.za
Breakerview (B)	Self Catering 039-315 7160 info@breakerview.co.za
Robin's Nest Bed & Breakfast (B)	Bed & Breakfast 039-315 0606 robin@robins-nest.co.za
Millar's Mansion (B)	Bed & Breakfast 039-315 1338 jason@millarsmansion.co.za
Port St Johns	
Tourism Information Office	047-564 1187 tourismpsj@wildcoast.co.za www.portstjohns.org.za
Scottburgh	
General contacts	www.scottburgh.kzn.org.za
Tourism Umdoni Coast and Country	039-976 1364 publicity@scottburgh.co.za www.scottburgh.co.za
Sodwana Bay	
Elephant Coast Tourism Association	035-562 0353 res@elephantcoastbookings.co.za www.elephantcoast.kzn.org.za
Southbroom	
Southbroom Tourism Bureau	039-316 6999 southbroom@hibiscuscoast.org.za www.southbroom.org.za
General contacts	www.southbroom.org
Southbroom Backpackers (A)	Backpackers 039-316 8448 urika@venturenet.co.za
Flamboyant (B)	Self Catering 082-3040 380 vanzyls2002@absamail.co.za
Bushbuck Lodge (B)	Self Catering 039-316 6399 polafrosafaris@ananzi.co.za
Sunny Rock (B)	Self Catering 039-316 8156 info@sunny-rock.co.za

CONTACTS

Golf House (B)	Bed & Breakfast 039-316 6982 info@golf-house.co.za
Southbroom Lodge (C)	Bed & Breakfast 039-316 8310 bookings@whiteshores.co.za
Whiteshores Guest House (C)	Bed & Breakfast 039-316 6534 pete@southbroomlodge.co.za
Hotel San Lameer/ Mondazur (C)	Hotel 039-313 0011 info@sl.mondazur.com
Sithela Country House (C)	Hotel 039-319 2773 stay@sithela.co.za
St Lucia	
Ezemvelo KZN Wildlife	033-845 1000 www.kznwildlife.com
St Lucia Tourism Bureau	035-590 1075/1777 info@stluciainfo.co.za www.stluciainfo.co.za
Elephant Coast Tourism Association	035-562 0353 res@elephantcoastbookings.co.za www.elephantcoast.kzn.org.za
Umkomaas & surrounds	
Heathton (B)	Self Catering 039-973 0603 tonybu@za.sappi.com
Annie's Retreat (B)	Self Catering 031-201 7667 bernardr@netsolutions.co.za
Casa Mia Guest House (B)	Bed & Breakfast 039-973 2170 info@casamia.co.za
Umkomaas Guest House (C)	Bed & Breakfast 039-973 1572 ugh@telkomsa.net
Ocean Park Guest House (B)	Bed & Breakfast 039-973 2657 oceanparkguesthouse@telkomsa.net
Ilfracombe Bed & Breakfast Association (B)	Bed & Breakfast 039-973 0983
Villa Mare (B)	Bed & Breakfast 039-973 2505 watersports@icon.co.za

Parks, museums, reserves and institutions			
Birds of Eden	08h00 to 17h00	044-5348706	R110 adults, R55 children (under 12) From Nov 2009 R120 adults R60 children	info@birdsofeden.co.za www.birdsofeden.co.za
Cango Caves	09h00 to 16h00 (Std tour) 09h30 to 15h30 (Adventure tour)	044-272 7410	R52 adults, R28 children (Std tour) R66 adults, R43 children (Adventure tour)	info@cangocaves.co.za www.cangocaves.co.za
Cape Columbine Nature Reserve	07h00 to 19h00	022-752 2718	R10 adults R7 children	
Cape Point Nature Reserve		021-780 9207	R60 per person, discounts for children under 12, free entry to Wildcard holders	
De Hoop Nature Reserve	07h00 to 18h00 (Fridays 19h00)	021-426 0723 021-423 9611		capenature@tourismcapetown.co.za www.capenature.org.za

Dias Museum	09h00 to 16h45 (Mon–Fri); 09h00 to 15h45 (weekends and public holidays)	044-691 1067		info@diasmuseum.co.za www.diasmuseum.co.za
Elephant Sanctuary	08h00 to 17h00	044-534 8145	R250 adults R125 children	crags@elephantsanctuary.co.za www.elephantsanctuary.co.za
Fernkloof Nature Reserve	08h30 to 12h00; Sundays 10h00 to 12h00	028-313 8200		www.fernkloof.com
Hoerikwaggo Trails		021-465 8515/9		
Monkey Land	08h00 to 17h00	044-5348906	R110 adults, R55 children (under 12) From Nov 2009 R120 adults R60 children	info@monkeyland.co.za
Nature's Valley	07h30 to 18h00	042-281 1607 044-631 6700	R25 SA residents R80 adults R40 children (non SA residents)	reservations@sanparks.org www.monkeyland.co.za www.parks-sa.co.za

Post Office Tree and Museum – Mossel Bay	09h00 to 16h45	044-6912202		admin@visitmosselbay.co.za www.visitmosselbay.co.za
Robben Island Ferry	Departs 09h00, 10h00, 12h00, 13h00, 14h00, 15h00 (weather permitting)	021-413 4208/9	Booking essential	
Rocherpan Nature Reserve	08h00 to 17h00 May to Aug	022-952 1727	R25 adults R12 children	www.capenature.co.za
	08h00 to 18h00 Sept to April			
Tsitsikamma Coastal National Park	07h00 to 19h00	042-281 1607		www.sanparks.org
Tsitsikamma Reserve	07h00 to 19h00	042-281 1607 042-280 3561	R25 SA residents R80 adults R40 children (non SA residents)	www.tsitsikamma.info

CONTACTS

Table Mountain Cableway	08h00 to 18h00 (Oct–April) 08h30 to 18h00 (May–Sept)		R130 adults R88 students R68 children (under 18) and senior citizens, R104 adult Wildcard holders R55 children Wildcard holders	
Table Mountain National Park			R55 adult R10 children	
Tokai Forest			R5 per person	
Two Oceans' Aquarium	09h30 to 18h00	021-418 3823	R76 adults R35 children 4–17 years, R60 pensioners and students	aquarium@aquarium.co.za www.aquarium.co.za
V&A Waterfront		021-408 7600		info@waterfront.co.za www.waterfront.co.za
Walker Bay Nature Reserve	Monday to Friday 08h00 to 16h00	021-426 0723 021-423 9611	Entry permit required. Obtain from gatehouse at De Kelders and Uilkraalsmond/ Walker Bay Nature Reserve office at Voëlklip	capenature@tourismcapetown.co.za www.capenature.org.za

West Coast National Park including Plankiesbaai and Langebaan	07h00 to 18h30 1 April to 30 Sept	022-7722144	**Outside of Flower Season** R20pp/day SA residents, R30 pp/day non SA residents	reservations@sanparks.org www.sanparks.org
	06h00 to 19h30 1 Oct to 31 March		**During Flower Season** R30pp/day (SA residents) R60 pp/day (non SA residents)	
Wildflower Festival		028-313 1992		
KwaZulu-Natal				
Hluhluwe National Park	Summer (Nov to Feb) 05h00 to 19h00, Winter (March to Oct) 06h00 to 18h00	035-562 0848	R45 adults R23 children (SA residents) R90 adults R45 children (non SA residents)	webmail@kznwildlife.com www.kznwildlife.com
Inanda Heritage Route	08h00 to 17h00			www.kzn.org.za

Imfolozi National Park	Summer (Nov to Feb) 05h00 to 19h00, Winter (March to Oct) 06h00 to 18h00	035-340 1836	R45 adults, R23 Children (SA residents) R90 adults R45 children (non SA residents)	webmail@kznwildlife.com www.kznwildlife.com
Natal Sharks Board	08h00 to 16h00 (Mon–Fri Display Hall & curio shop) Shows Tues–Thurs 09h00 & 14h00, Sun 14h00	031-566 0400	R25 adults, R12 children and senior citizens (audio-visual presentation followed by shark dissection) 09h00 to 14h00 Tues–Thurs Phone for group bookings	www.shark.co.za
Natal Sharks Board Boat Trip	Departs 06h30	082-403 9206	R200	
Ndumo Reserve	06h00 to 18h00 Winter, 06h00 to 19h00 Summer	035-591 0058	R35 adults R20 children + R35 per vehicle	webmail@kznwildlife.com www.kznwildlife.com

Ocean Safaris	08h00 to 17h00 Cruises run from 12h00 to 14h30	084-565 5328 044-533 4963	Premium cruise: R500 adults R300 children Discovery cruise: R300 adults R150 children	info@airandoceansafaris.co.za info@oceansafaris.co.za www.oceansafaris.co.za
Sodwana Bay	24 Hours	035-571 0051/2	R20 adults R15 children	webmail@kznwildlife.com www.kznwildlife.com
St Lucia/iSimangaliso Wetland Park	05h00 to 19h00 (from 1 Nov) 06h00 to18h00 (from 1 April)	035-590 1340 033-845 1000	R20 adults R10 children	webmail@kznwildlife.com www.kznwildlife.com
Tala Reserve	07h00 to 18h00	031-781 8000	R30 adults R20 children + R40 per vehicle	info@tala.co.za www.tala.co.za
uShaka Sea World	09h00 to 18h00	031-328 8000	R98 adults R66 children	mkt@ushakamarineworld.co.za www.ushakamarineworld.co.za
uShaka Wet 'n Wild	09h00 to 18h00 (Wed to Sun)	031-328 8000	R98 adults R66 children	mkt@ushakamarineworld.co.za www.ushakamarineworld.co.za

References/further reading

Ashton, N. 2006. *The Whales of Walker Bay.* International Fund for Animal Welfare.

BBC News. 18 November 2007. 'Japanese Whalers Hunt Humpbacks.' www.bbc.co.uk.

Best, P. B. 2008. *Whales and Dolphins of the Southern African Subregion.* Cambridge University Press.

Best, P. B. 1995. *Whale Watching in South Africa.* The Mammal Research Institute, University of Pretoria.

Best, P. B. 1995. *Whale Watching Along the Southern African Coast.* Mammal Research Institute, University of Pretoria.

Bryson, B. 2003. *A Short History of Nearly Everything.* Doubleday, London.

Chadwick, D. H. November 2001. 'The Evolution of Whales' in *The National Geographic.*

Conroy, E. The Associated Press. June 2007. 'Alaska Bowhead Whale Taken This Year Held Century-old Harpoon Head' in *The Anchorage Daily News.*

Davies, G. H. 1995. 'How David Attenborough Made Trials of Life' in *The Radio Times.*

Dolphin Action and Protection Group. March 1999. *Strip Mining the Oceans.* Dolphin Action and Protection Group Information Sheet 027. Cape Town.

Dolphin Action and Protection Group. September 1999. *Dolphins should be Free.* Dolphin Action and Protection Group Information Sheet 502. Cape Town.

Dolphin Action and Protection Group. September 1999. *Heaviside's Dolphin.* Dolphin Action and Protection Group Information Sheet 503. Cape Town.

Dolphin Action and Protection Group. April 2001. *The Dusky Dolphin.* Dolphin Action and Protection Group Information Sheet 506. Cape Town.

Dolphin Action and Protection Group. November 2002. *The Bryde's Whale.* Dolphin Action and Protection

Group Information Sheet J09. Cape Town.

Dolphin Action and Protection Group. November 2002. *The Minke Whale.* Dolphin Action and Protection Group Information Sheet 014. Cape Town.

Dolphin Action and Protection Group. November 2002. *The Plight of Small Cetaceans.* Dolphin Action and Protection Group Information Sheet 026. Cape Town.

Dolphin Action and Protection Group. July 2003. *Blue Whale.* Dolphin Action and Protection Group Information Sheet. Cape Town.

Dolphin Action and Protection Group. July 2003. *Humpback Whale.* Dolphin Action and Protection Group Information Sheet D3. Cape Town.

Dolphin Action and Protection Group. July 2003. *Killer Whale.* Dolphin Action and Protection Group Information Sheet 023. Cape Town.

Dolphin Action and Protection Group. July 2003. *Save the Whales.* Dolphin Action and Protection Group Information Sheet J12. Cape Town.

Dolphin Action and Protection Group. July 2003. *Some Facts about Dolphins and Whales.* Dolphin Action and Protection Group Information Sheet D2. Cape Town.

Dolphin Action and Protection Group. July 2003. *The Great White Shark.* Dolphin Action and Protection Group Information Sheet 504. Cape Town.

Dolphin Action and Protection Group. July 2004. *Coastal Marine Pollution—how it affects Cetaceans.* Dolphin Action and Protection Group Information Sheet. Cape Town.

Dolphin Action and Protection Group. July 2004. *The Southern Right Whale.* Dolphin Action and Protection Group Information Sheet 013. Cape Town.

Dolphin Action and Protection Group. Undated. *Dolphin or Porpoise—which is which?* Dolphin Action and Protection Group Information Sheet. Cape Town.

Dolphin Action and Protection Group. Undated.

Dolphins—the facts. Dolphin Action and Protection Group Information Sheet 002. Cape Town.

Dolphin Action and Protection Group. Undated. *Purse-Seining on Dolphins—Eastern Tropical Pacific.* Dolphin Action and Protection Group Information Sheet 016. Cape Town.

Du Toit, S. J. 2005. *Hermanus Stories 1.* ABC Press, Cape Town.

Edey, M. A. (ed.). 1969. *The Sea.* Life Nature Library. Time Inc, Netherlands.

Garden Route Marketing. 2007. *Cape Town, Winelands, Route 62, Overberg, West Coast, Namibia—Your Travel Companion.* Garden Route Marketing.

Garden Route Marketing. 2007. *Garden Route Klein Karoo Route 62—Your Travel Companion.* 13th Edition. Garden Route Marketing.

McCarthy, T. and Rubidge, B. 2005. *The Story of Earth and Life—A southern African perspective on a 4.6 billion year journey.* Struik, Cape Town.

Nel, J. January 1999. 'On the Whale Trail' in *Getaway.*

Squires, N. November 2007. 'Greens and Governments Condemn Whale Hunt.' www.telegraph.co.uk.

Turnbull, D. L. 'Dolphins and Whales in Mythology: Part one of a multidisciplinary unit.' Yale–New Haven Teachers Institute. www.yale.edu.

Weaver, T. June 1996. 'Whale of a Time' in *Living Africa.*

Useful websites/contacts

o www.fossilguy.com – Washington University
o www.pbs
o www.wikipedia.com
o www.theoi.com/ther/ketea.htm
o www.greenpeace.org
o www.whaleroute.com
o www.edwardtbabinski.us/whales
o www.whalingmuseum.org
o www.neoucom.edu
o www.iwcoffice.org

Information on whales, their habits, migration routes and origins, as well as local history

o www.ifaw.org – IFAW South Africa
o www.dolphinstudies.co.za – Centre for Dolphin Studies
o www.up.ac.za/academic/zoology/mri – Mammal Research Institute
o www.sharkattacks.com – shark attack information
o www.luna.pos.to/whale/icr_rw_kasa.html – counting whales in the Antarctic
o www.oceansofafrica.co.za – Noel Ashton's Oceans of Africa and Studio
o www.shark.co.za – Natal Sharks Board
o www.sanbi.org – SA Biodiversity Institute
o www.dolphintrail.co.za – The Dolphin Trail
o www.iwcoffice.co.za – International Whaling Commission
o www.neoucom.edu – whale evolution
o www.africaimagery.com – Africa Imagery
o www.30degreessouth.co.za – 30° South Publishers
o www.news.nationalgeographic.com – National Geographic

- o www.slipway.co.za – historical whaling at Saldanha
- o www.fad.co.za – whaling history of Durban
- o www.danger-point-peninsula.co.za – Danger Point and the *Birkenhead*
- o http://battlefields.kzn.org.za – KZN battlefields

Boat-based whale watching and marine life safari operators

Cape

- o www.waterfrontboats.co.za – Waterfront boat trips
- o www.boatcompany.co.za – Simon's Town boat company
- o www.whalewatchingsa.co.za/www.whaleviewing.co.za – Ivanhoe Sea Safaris
- o www.southernrightcharters.co.za – Southern Right Charters
- o www.hermanus-whale-cruises.co.za – Hermanus Whale Cruises
- o www.whalewatchsa.com – Dyer Island Cruises
- o www.mosselbay.co.za/romonza – Romonza Boat Trips
- o www.oceansafaris.co.za – Ocean Safaris
- o www.oceanadventures.co.za – Ocean Blue Adventures

KwaZulu-Natal

- o www.advantagetours.co.za – Advantage Charters
- o www.airandoceansafaris.co.za – Ocean Safaris Durban

KwaZulu-Natal tourist information

- o http://durban.kzn.org – Durban Tourism
- o www.durban.gov.za – Durban Metro
- o www.sardinerun.com – South Coast sardine run
- o www.ushakamarineworld.co.za – uShaka Marine World

- o www.hibiscuscoast.kzn.org.za – KZN South Coast
- o www.umhlanga-rocks.com – Umhlanga Tourism
- o www.1000hills.kzn.org.za – Valley of 1,000 Hills
- o http://southcoast.kzn.org.za – KZN South Coast
- o http://dolphincoast.kzn.org.za – KZN North Coast
- o http://pmb-midlands.kzn.org.za – Pietermaritzburg Tourism
- o www.zulu.org.za – KZN and Zululand
- o www.zulucountry.co.za – Drakensberg and Midlands
- o http://drakensberg.kzn.org.za – Drakensberg
- o http://zululand.kzn.org.za – Zululand
- o http://elephantcoast.kzn.org.za – northern KZN
- o www.oldcanvasexpeditions.com – Old Canvas Expeditions

KwaZulu-Natal wildlife reserves and institutions

- o www.isimangaliso.com – iSimangaliso (St Lucia) Wetland Park
- o www.kznwildlife.com – KZN-Ezemvelo Wildlife

Cape tourist information

- o www.overberginfo.com – Overberg Tourist Information
- o www.tourismcapetown.co.za – Cape Town Tourism
- o www.hermanus.co.za – Hermanus Tourism
- o www.overberg.co.za – Overberg Tourism
- o www.oceansafaris.co.za – Ocean Safaris, Plettenberg Bay
- o www.tablemountain.net – Table Mountain Cableway
- o www.waterfront.co.za – Cape Town Waterfront
- o www.capecraftanddesign.org.za – Cape Craft and Design
- o www.robben-island.org.net – Robben Island
- o www.aquarium.co.za – Two Oceans Aquarium

- www.tourismgardenroute.co.za – Garden Route Tourism
- www.tourismcapeoverberg.co.za – Overberg Tourism
- www.tourismcapewestcoast.co.za – West Coast Tourism
- www.tourismcentralkaroo.co.za – Karoo Tourism
- www.swellendamtourism.co.za – Swellendam Tourism
- www.witsandtourism.co.za – Witsand Tourism
- www.tourismheidelberg.co.za – Heidelberg Tourism
- www.tourismriversdale.co.za – Riversdale Tourism
- www.stilbaaitourism.com – Stilbaai Tourism
- www.visitmosselbay.co.za – Mossel Bay
- www.tourismgeorge.co.za – George Tourism
- www.tourismwilderness.co.za – Wilderness Tourism
- www.tourismsedgefield.co.za – Sedgefield Tourism
- www.tourismknysna.co.za – Knysna Tourism
- www.plettenbergbay.co.za – Plettenberg Bay Tourism
- www.treetoptour.co.za – Tsitsikamma Tourism
- www.derust.co.za – De Rust Tourism
- www.patourism.co.za – Prince Albert Tourism
- www.tourismbeaufortwest.co.za – Beaufort West
- www.oudtshoorn.com – Oudtshoorn Tourism
- www.calitzdorp.co.za – Calitzdorp Tourism
- www.barrydale.co.za – Barrydale Tourism
- www.ladismith.org.za – Ladismith Tourism
- www.yourtravelcompanion.co.za – Your Travel Companion
- www.tourismmontagu.co.za – Montagu Tourism

Cape wildlife reserves and institutions

- www.birdsofeden.co.za – Birds of Eden, Plettenberg Bay
- www.monkeyland.co.za – Monkey Land, Plettenberg Bay
- http://www.capenature.org.za – CapeNature

o www.sanparks.org – Karoo National Park
o www.sanparks.org – Garden Route National Parks
o www.cangocaves.co.za – The Cango Caves
o www.capenature.co.za – Anysberg Nature Reserve

General accommodation websites

o www.hermanusaccommodation.co.za – Hermanus
accommodation
o www.sleepafrica.com – Hermanus accommodation
o www.wheretostay.co.za – Where To Stay—national
accommodation site
o www.safarinow.com – Safari Inn—national
accommodation site
o www.roomsforafrica.com – Rooms for Africa—
national accommodation site
o www.accommodationsouthafrica.co.za
– Accommodation South Africa—national
accommodation site
o www.sleeping-out.co.za – Sleeping Out—national
accommodation site
o www.coastingafrica.com – Coast to Coast
backpackers' guide
o www.alternativeroute.net – The Alternative Route
backpackers' guide

Index

Acknowledgements

Thanks must go firstly to Chris and Kerrin Cocks who had the faith to allow me to write this book, based on a few emails and a single telephone conversation. Thanks must also go to Professor Best of the IMR who sacrificed a Friday morning to talk about whales and reminisce about old-time whalers. Dr Vic Cockcroft also took time out to discuss the politics of whales, of which there are not a few, and Nan Rice's contributions in terms of literature and conservation were invaluable. Roger de la Harpe pulled some strings with his wide range of contacts in the tourism industry, which opened a number of doors to us in the Cape. Thanks too must go to Stephanie Shrosbree of Plettenberg Bay who assisted us immensely when we were there. Thanks too, to Shane and Lara of Monkey Land and Birds of Eden and Louise at the Elephant Sanctuary, as well as Charlie of Ocean Safaris. Soné of Dyer Island, we never got to see you, but thanks for the information pack sent subsequently. Pamela Le Noury of Ocean Safaris saved the day in terms of East Coast operators and information. Then there are those unknown contributors to Wikipedia and those myriad websites whose information provided a basic understanding of ceteology and whale evolution, all of which is impossible to acknowledge in a way that is both practical and meaningful—to them all I must extend my heartfelt thanks—I stand on the shoulders of giants. And finally, to André and Carmen, who made the Cape trip memorable and supplied support, meals and an ongoing supply of tea during weekends and long evenings when this book was only in its nascent form.